The Civil War

Other books in the Turning Points series:

Turning Points

IN WORLD HISTORY

The Civil War

James Tackach, *Book Editor*

Bruce Glassman, *Vice President*
Bonnie Szumski, *Publisher*
Helen Cothran, *Managing Editor*

GREENHAVEN
PRESS®

THOMSON

━━━━✦━━━━
™
GALE

San Diego • Detroit • New York • San Francisco • Cleveland
New Haven, Conn. • Waterville, Maine • London • Munich

For more information, contact
Greenhaven Press
27500 Drake Rd.
Farmington Hills, MI 48331-3535
Or you can visit our Internet site at http://www.gale.com

Cover credits: © Medford Historical Society Collection/CORBIS
Library of Congress, 45, 55, 64, 71, 95, 103, 119, 126
National Archives, 57

LIBRARY OF CONGRESS CATALOGING-IN-PUBLICATION DATA

The Civil War / James Tackach, book editor.
    p. cm. — (Turning points in world history)
    Includes bibliographical references and index.
    ISBN 0-7377-1114-0 (lib. : alk. paper)
      1. United States—History—Civil War, 1861–1865. I. Tackach, James. II. Turning points in world history (Greenhaven Press)
    E468.C614 2004
    973.7—dc22   2003064297

Contents

Chapter 1: A Nation Divides: The Causes of the Civil War

Chapter 2: Early Battlefield Victories and the Prospect of European Intervention Fuel the South's Hope for Independence

Foreword

Certain past events stand out as pivotal, as having effects and outcomes that change the course of history. These events are often referred to as turning points. Historian Louis L. Snyder provides this useful definition:

> A turning point in history is an event, happening, or stage which thrusts the course of historical development into a different direction. By definition a turning point is a great event, but it is even more—a great event with the explosive impact of altering the trend of man's life on the planet.

History's turning points have taken many forms. Some were single, brief, and shattering events with immediate and obvious impact. The invasion of Britain by William the Conqueror in 1066, for example, swiftly transformed that land's political and social institutions and paved the way for the rise of the modern English nation. By contrast, other single events were deemed of minor significance when they occurred, only later recognized as turning points. The assassination of a little-known European nobleman, Archduke Franz Ferdinand, on June 28, 1914, in the Bosnian town of Sarajevo was such an event; only after it touched off a chain reaction of political-military crises that escalated into the global conflict known as World War I did the murder's true significance become evident.

Other crucial turning points occurred not in terms of a few hours, days, months, or even years, but instead as evolutionary developments spanning decades or even centuries. One of the most pivotal turning points in human history, for instance—the development of agriculture, which replaced nomadic hunter-gatherer societies with more permanent settlements—occurred over the course of many generations. Still other great turning points were neither events nor developments, but rather revolutionary new inventions and innovations that significantly altered social customs and ideas, military tactics, home life, the spread of knowledge, and the human condition in general. The developments of writing, gunpowder, the printing press, antibiotics, the electric light, atomic energy, television, and the computer, the last two of which have recently ushered in the world-altering information age, represent only some of these innovative turning points.

Each anthology in the Greenhaven Turning Points in World History series presents a group of essays chosen for their accessibility. The anthology's structure also enhances this accessibility. First, an introductory essay provides a general overview of the principal events and figures involved, placing the topic in its historical context. The essays that follow explore various aspects in more detail, some targeting political trends and consequences, others social, literary, cultural, and/or technological ramifications, and still others pivotal leaders and other influential figures. To aid the reader in choosing the material of immediate interest or need, each essay is introduced by a concise summary of the contributing writer's main themes and insights.

In addition, each volume contains extensive research tools, including a collection of excerpts from primary source documents pertaining to the historical events and figures under discussion. In the anthology on the French Revolution, for example, readers can examine the works of Rousseau, Voltaire, and other writers and thinkers whose championing of human rights helped fuel the French people's growing desire for liberty; the French *Declaration of the Rights of Man and Citizen*, presented to King Louis XVI by the French National Assembly on October 2, 1789; and eyewitness accounts of the attack on the royal palace and the horrors of the Reign of Terror. To guide students interested in pursuing further research on the subject, each volume features an extensive bibliography, which for easy access has been divided into separate sections by topic. Finally, a comprehensive index allows readers to scan and locate content efficiently. Each of the anthologies in the Greenhaven Turning Points in World History series provides students with a complete, detailed, and enlightening examination of a crucial historical watershed.

Introduction: The United States *Is*

On June 16, 1858, Abraham Lincoln of Illinois kicked off his campaign for a seat in the United States Senate with a powerful speech, arguably the most important oration of his prepresidential career. Candidate Lincoln, who knew the Bible well, composed his address around a passage from the New Testament: "A house divided against itself cannot stand. I believe this government cannot endure, permanently half *slave* and half *free*. I do not expect the Union to be *dissolved*— I do not expect the house to *fall*—but I *do* expect it will cease to be divided. It will become *all* one thing, or *all* the other."[1]

Lincoln biographer Don E. Fehrenbacher calls Lincoln's "House Divided" speech "one of those moments of synthesis which embody the past and illume the future."[2] Indeed Lincoln's biblical metaphor accurately described the condition of the United States in the middle of the nineteenth century: The eighty-two-year-old nation had become a house divided, a country rigidly separated into two distinct regions, North and South. But in this speech, Lincoln also foresaw the dramatic events of the next decade. Lincoln scholars have debated whether Lincoln was actually prophesizing a civil war between the North and South over slavery when he described his nation as a house divided in the late spring of 1858. Lincoln certainly sensed, however, that the day would soon come when his country would no longer be divided; its disparate parts—North and South, East and West—would be fused into a singular entity, a true Union, an undivided nation, rather than a loosely joined collection of states. The event that would initiate this fusion would be a climactic civil war—sometimes called the Second American Revolution—that would commence three years after Lincoln delivered his House Divided address and just one month after Lincoln assumed the office of president of the United States. The Civil War, a devastating conflict waged from 1861 through 1865, was a major turning point in American history; it eradicated the main cause for division between North and South—slavery—and began a long process of unifying the divided house.

Forming a Nation from Independent States

The United States of America was a house divided at its birth. Its birth certificate—the Declaration of Independence—boldly asserted that as of July 4, 1776, Great Britain's thirteen American colonies, united in their opposition to the rule of their parent country, "are, and of Right, ought to be *Free and Independent States.*" When the colonies officially won their independence in 1783, they essentially became thirteen independent political entities with separate governments and laws, individual currencies, and independent militias. These thirteen states were not yet a nation.

The delegates to the Philadelphia Convention of 1787 attempted to mold the thirteen newly freed states into a union. The main result of that convention was the creation of a constitution that knitted the thirteen states into a republic with a centralized federal government that would rule the land. The Preamble to the Constitution of the United States of America clearly stated the document's most fundamental goal: "to form a more perfect union."

The United States Constitution, which was ratified in 1788 and went into effect a year later, created a political union of states, but that document could not by itself unite the states economically or culturally. The new nation covered a vast mass of land, from frigid New England to the balmy Carolinas and Georgia. In the Northeast, an urban economy was developing around three great cities—Philadelphia, New York, and Boston—while the Southern states remained agricultural, and the nation's western reaches comprised rugged frontier land. In 1789, no central means of communication or transportation existed to bind the individual regions and states. The steamboat, telegraph, and railroad had not yet been invented, and mail service from state to state was slow and less than perfectly reliable. Newspapers were mainly local, not national, in their focus. Given the size of the new American republic and the absence of technological devices that would tie citizens from one region to those of another, it is hardly surprising that the different regions of the country would develop separate economies, separate political identities, and separate cultural traditions.

Perhaps the most obvious division within the new nation was the one that formed along what became known as the Mason-Dixon Line, named after two surveyors who traced the boundary between Maryland and Pennsylvania during the 1790s. The Mason-Dixon Line eventually developed into the rigid border between the Northern states and the Southern states, the so-called free states and the slave states.

Slavery Develops in America

The first slaves—captured black Africans—came to America in 1619. During the next century, thousands of black Africans were brought against their will to the American colonies and turned into slaves. Most slaves remained in bondage for the duration of their lives, and their offspring were born into perpetual slavery. During the seventeenth century, slavery spread to all of Great Britain's American colonies, north and south. In the agricultural economy that developed in America during the seventeenth century, slaves would become valuable possessions. With very little training, they could learn to plow a field, sow seed, harvest crops, build fences and walls, tend livestock, and perform other duties required in an agricultural economy.

During the mid-eighteenth century, however, slavery began to disappear in the Northern colonies. The North's shorter growing season prompted the need for a more diversified economy. The South, with its longer growing season, could depend on agriculture as its economic backbone, but the North could not. Hence, an urban economy of tradesmen, craftsmen, and shopkeepers developed in the larger cities of the North. As this urban economy developed, the need for slaves decreased sharply. Training unskilled slaves to work in the North's dynamic and diversified economy was expensive and time-consuming. Moreover, Northerners who remained in farming could not afford to feed, clothe, and house slaves for eight months so that the slaves could work in the fields during the four-month growing season. It was cheaper for Northern farmers to employ day laborers during the growing season rather than possess slaves.

When the colonies declared their independence from Great Britain during the summer of 1776, a rift between the Northern and Southern colonies over slavery had already developed. The original draft of the Declaration of Independence, written by Thomas Jefferson, contained a severe indictment of slavery. Jefferson accused King George III of Great Britain of waging "a cruel war against human nature itself, violating its most sacred right of life and liberty in the persons of a distant people who never offended him, captivating them into slavery in another hemisphere, or to incur miserable death in their transportation thither."[3] But the Southern delegates to the Continental Congress objected to that clause in the Declaration of Independence; they could not condemn the British monarch for an institution that played a vital role in their region's economy. Although the final draft of the Declaration asserted that "all men are created" and "are endowed by their Creator with certain inalienable rights," including "life, liberty, and the pursuit of happiness," slavery would not be a casualty of America's war for independence.

Slavery in the New American Republic

When representatives from the thirteen newly independent colonies gathered in Philadelphia in 1787 to draft the United States Constitution, five Northern colonies had already passed emancipation laws that immediately or gradually abolished slavery. The membership of the Pennsylvania Antislavery Society urged Benjamin Franklin, a Pennsylvania delegate to the Philadelphia Convention, to include a clause in the new constitution that would abolish slavery, but Franklin, sensing the Southern delegates' strong opposition to the idea, never formally introduced an antislavery measure at the convention. The new constitution would contain an article that recognized slaves as property. Section 2 of Article IV states, *"no person held to service or labor in one State, under the laws thereof, escaping into another, shall, in consequence of any law or regulation therein, be discharged from such service or labor, but shall be delivered up on claim of the party to whom such service or labor may be due.*" In short, this article enabled slaveholders to retrieve runaway slaves by asserting property rights.

By 1804, all of the states north of the Mason-Dixon Line had passed laws to abolish slavery, but slavery was becoming even more deeply embedded in the South's culture and economy. In 1793, Eli Whitney, a New Englander, had secured a patent for a machine that quickly removed the seeds from freshly picked balls of cotton. Whitney's cotton gin, which mechanized a labor-intensive process that previously had been done by hand, turned cotton into a cash crop. The South's climate was perfect for cotton farming, and the laborious tasks of planting, tending, and harvesting cotton could be performed by unskilled slaves. Ambitious Southern landowners could raise a cotton crop, readily turn that crop into cash, and use the cash to buy more slaves and land. In the opening decades of the nineteenth century, cotton became the South's most profitable crop for domestic sale and export, and slave labor remained critical to the business of raising and selling cotton.

As the South developed into a kingdom of cotton, the North became more industrialized. By 1800, the Industrial Revolution, which had its roots in Great Britain during the late-eighteenth century, had crossed the Atlantic Ocean and arrived in America. Throughout the North, mills were erected to create products that had been previously imported. Northerners began to demand high tariffs on imported products to encourage Americans to purchase cheaper, domestically produced goods. Southerners opposed these tariffs, preferring the ability to purchase cheap imported goods rather than subsidize the North's growing industries. Tariffs became another issue of contention between the North and the South.

Two Cultures

The economic differences between North and South that developed at the turn of the nineteenth century paralleled cultural differences between the two regions. As the Civil

War-era historian Bruce Catton suggests, the South in the nineteenth century became "a static society which could endure almost anything except change"; Southerners believed in "a leisure class, backed by ownership of land."[4] Landownership and its privileges were passed down from father to son, creating a stable and permanent aristocratic class that would dominate the region economically, politically, and culturally. The North, however, developed into a region characterized by rapid change and inhabited by self-made individuals. In the North, social mobility was more evident than in the South. The children of impoverished immigrants could work hard, acquire capital, and make their mark in the world. Abraham Lincoln articulated this idea in a speech delivered in Kalamazoo, Michigan, in 1856. Southerners "think that men are always to remain laborers here—but there is no such class," stated Lincoln. "That man who labored for another last year, this year labors for himself, and next year he will hire others to labor for him."[5]

Thus, the South developed into a society that looked backward to the age of European feudalism, when a small number of lords owned large tracks of land and the majority of citizens toiled to maintain the lord's properties. The North, in contrast, looked forward to an age of industry and technology; it developed into a dynamic, progressive region where an individual like Lincoln, born into a family of poor and illiterate frontier farmers, could become a well-to-do lawyer and successful politician. Northerners like Lincoln opposed slavery, in part, because it negated the individual's right to rise, to seize the opportunity to exceed far beyond his or her parents' circumstances, while most Southerners embraced the idea of a permanently established aristocratic class that would be served by a working class and slaves.

An Era of Good Feeling

Despite their cultural and economic differences, and occasional disputes over tariffs or slavery, the North and South remained at peace during the first three decades of the nineteenth century. The new nation prospered. It acquired land via the Louisiana Purchase of 1803 and defended itself in a war against Great Britain in 1812. American pioneers spread westward across the American continent and conquered the frontier.

One reason for this so-called "era of good feeling" was an unstated agreement between the North and the South over the main issue that divided the nation—slavery. Northerners agreed not to attempt to uproot slavery in Southern states and territories where it already existed. Even Northerners like Lincoln who objected to slavery on moral grounds understood its importance to the South's economy, and they realized that the institution was protected by the United States Constitution. Southerners, in turn, agreed not to endeavor to introduce slavery in the North, where it had essentially been abolished by state law. Due to this agreement, these two economically and culturally different regions were able to coexist fairly harmoniously in one nation.

But the house would eventually begin to divide, and the energy for division was provided by the settlement of the Western territories. During the first two decades of the nineteenth century, American pioneers streamed into the new territory acquired through the Louisiana Purchase. When the Constitution went into effect in 1789, the United States comprised thirteen states—the same thirteen colonies that had achieved independence from Great Britain. Thirty years later, in 1819, the Union consisted of twenty-two states. Seven of the original thirteen states were or became free states that outlawed slavery. Five of the next nine states admitted to the Union were slave states, carved out of territory south of the Mason-Dixon Line. In December 1819, when Alabama achieved statehood, the Union consisted of eleven free states and eleven slave states, a balance that enabled the North and South to coexist peacefully in the same nation. Missouri's request for admission to the Union late in 1819 threatened to disrupt that delicate balance.

The Missouri Crisis

Since 1790, nine territories had joined the Union as states with little rancor or debate in Congress. The question of slavery had already been settled in these territories before their admission to the Union. Slaves already existed in large numbers in Kentucky, Tennessee, Louisiana, Mississippi, and Alabama when they applied for statehood. Moreover, these territories were all south of the Mason-Dixon Line. When they entered the Union, they drew up state constitutions that allowed slavery. On the other hand, Vermont, Ohio, Indiana, and Illinois had no tradition of slavery when they entered the Union, and all became free states.

Missouri's request for admission to the Union in 1819, however, opened a national debate on slavery that would not be settled completely until the Civil War. Many Northerners argued that Congress had the right to prohibit slavery in a new state; Southerners disagreed, asserting that a state could choose for itself whether to allow or prohibit slavery. Missouri already contained slaves, and its citizens lobbied to enter the Union as a slave state, but Northerners feared that adding a slave state would give the South the advantage in the United States Senate, which at the time of Missouri's application for statehood was evenly divided between senators from free states and senators from slave states. Antislavery Northerners contended that the nation's Founding Fathers had not intended slavery to spread to new states and territories.

As the debate over Missouri's statehood intensified, a handful of congressmen worked out a compromise. Missouri would be added to the Union as a slave state, and Maine would enter the Union as a free sate, preserving the delicate balance between free and slave states. In addition, slavery would be excluded from any United States territory north of the 36°30' latitude mark. This agreement, known as the Missouri Compromise or the Compromise of 1820, resolved the tense debate over Missouri's statehood, but it widened the rift between North and South over slavery that had existed since the signing of the Declaration of Independence. Thomas Jefferson, retired from politics at the time of the passage of the Missouri Compromise, lamented in a letter to a friend the widening rift that was developing between the North and the South. "A geographical line, coinciding with a marked principle, moral and political, once conceived and held up to the angry passions of men, will never be obliterated; and every new irritation will mark it deeper and deeper."[6]

Jefferson was correct. The debate over Missouri's statehood had sparked a national debate about slavery that would elevate tensions between the two regions. The era of good feeling between North and South was over. During the next forty years, as Jefferson predicted, the nation would split apart, and slavery would become the wedge that would divide the nation and ultimately cause a civil war.

The Abolitionist Crusade

Abolitionist voices existed in the United States before the passage of the Missouri Compromise, but those voices were not unified in any national movement. The Missouri legislation, however, prompted American abolitionists to voice a more forceful condemnation of Southern slavery. In 1829, David Walker, a free African American, published *Walker's Appeal in Four Acts*, an antislavery pamphlet that prophesized God's vengeance on the United States for the sin of slavery. *Walker's Appeal* was the first of many abolitionist texts that would flood the publishing market during the next decade. In 1833, John Greenlief Whittier, a Massachusetts poet, published an abolitionist pamphlet titled *Justice and Expediency: Or Slavery Considered with a View to Its Rightful and Effectual Remedy, Abolition*. Theodore Weld's influential abolitionist book, *American Slavery As It Is: The Testimony of a Thousand Witnesses*, appeared in 1839.

Many historians, however, consider January 1, 1831, as the birth date of the American abolitionist movement. On that date, William Lloyd Garrison, a Massachusetts abolitionist, published the first edition of *The Liberator*, an abolitionist newspaper that would continue until 1865. The main editorial in the inaugural edition of *The Liberator* boldly asserted Garrison's purpose: "I shall strenuously contend for the immediate enfranchisement of our slave population. . . . I am in earnest—I will not equivocate—I will not excuse—I will not retreat a single inch—AND I WILL BE HEARD."[7]

Garrison championed an abolitionist movement that gained momentum during the 1830s. In 1833, he helped establish the American Anti-Slavery Society, whose charter declared that all laws "admitting the right of slavery" are "before God utterly null and void."[8] Garrison's crusade attracted authors like Whittier and Henry David Thoreau; clergymen like William Ellery Channing, Theodore Parker, and Lyman Beecher; and women's rights activists such as Lydia Maria Child and Angelina and Sarah Grimké.

The rise of a national abolitionist movement prompted Southerners to defend slavery with renewed vigor. After Nat Turner's Rebellion, a slave revolt that occurred in Southampton County, Virginia, in the summer of 1831, several Southern states indicted Garrison for inciting the rebellion. In November 1837, proslavery Missourians crossed the Ohio River into Illinois and killed Reverend Elijah Lovejoy, an abolitionist editor, and destroyed his printing presses. Tensions between North and South increased. Garrison and some of his lieutenants began to argue that the North should secede from the Union and establish a separate slave-free nation.

The Slavery Debate Intensifies

By the 1840s, every national debate erupted into a conflict between the North and South over slavery. When the United States went to war with Mexico in 1846, antislavery Northerners accused President James Polk of trying to acquire more slave territory for the nation. Even before that two-year conflict ended, Representative David Wilmot proposed a bill stipulating that slavery would be prohibited in any new territory acquired by the United States during the war. Wilmot's bill, called the Wilmot Proviso, passed in the House of Representatives but was defeated by Southerners in the Senate.

The issue of slavery in new states and territories further split the North and South. The discovery of gold in California in 1849 resulted in thousands of new California residents. When California applied for statehood in September 1849, the congressional debate over statehood again turned into a debate over slavery. Early in 1850, New Mexico also applied for statehood, and both New Mexico and California wished to enter the Union as free states. Southern legislators balked at the addition of two new free states to the Union, but Congress avoided a national crisis by forging another compromise—the Compromise of 1850. The agreement allowed California to enter the Union as a free state, postponed statehood for New Mexico until its citizens could vote on the slavery issue, outlawed the slave trade in the District of Columbia, and enacted a tough Fugitive Slave Law that mandated federal assistance in the capture of runaway slaves.

The compromise averted the crisis brought on by California's application for statehood, but it angered abolitionists, who vigorously objected to the Fugitive Slave Law. Reverend Theodore Parker, a Boston abolitionist clergyman, announced to his congregation that he would break the Fugitive Slave Law if he had the opportunity to aid an escaped slave. Thoreau asserted that the Fugitive Slave Law "rises not to the level of the head; its natural habitat is the dirt. It was born and bred, and has its life only in the dust and mire . . . so trample it under foot."[9] After the enactment of the Fugitive Slave Law, Harriet Beecher Stowe wrote to her sister-in-law that "the time is come when even a woman or a child who can speak for freedom and humanity is bound to speak."[10] Stowe spoke forcefully. She immediately began work on the greatest and most effective piece of antislavery literature— the novel *Uncle Tom's Cabin*. The book would be a runaway best-seller in the North and would be banned in the South.

The Kansas Crisis

The Compromise of 1850 did not buy a stable peace between North and South. Another crisis arose in 1854 when the Kansas-Nebraska territory applied for statehood. Again the debate in Congress over the territory's statehood turned into a standoff between Northern and Southern legislators over slavery. After weeks of intense debate, Senator Stephen Douglas of Illinois proposed a resolution that garnered the necessary support for passage. The territory would be divided into two separate states, Kansas and Nebraska, and the citizens of each territory would vote on the question of slavery before admission to the Union.

After the passage of the Kansas-Nebraska Act, proslavery and antislavery settlers streamed into Kansas. Inevitably, violence broke out between the two factions, and Kansas became known as "Bleeding Kansas." More than two hundred Kansan settlers lost their lives in this civil war before federal troops arrived in 1856 to establish peace in the territory. Americans had now killed Americans over the issue of slavery.

The Kansas-Nebraska debate prompted the formation of a new political party, the Republicans, dedicated to curtailing the spread of slavery. The Republicans, Lincoln's party, would play a major role in the events leading to the Civil War.

On the Road Toward War

During the late 1850s, the rift between North and South became irreparable; as Lincoln suggested, the American house divided. In 1857, the United States Supreme Court's decision in the *Dred Scott* case moved the North and South closer to war. Scott, a Missouri slave, was taken by his master, John Emerson, to reside in the free territory of Minnesota and the free state of Illinois. After Emerson's death, Scott sued for his freedom, arguing that he had become a free man while residing in a free territory and free state. The Supreme Court rejected Scott's bid for freedom, asserting that a slave is a piece of property that remains in its owner's possession when the owner crosses state lines. The decision troubled Northerners. If a slave owner can take one slave into free territory and retain possession of that slave, what would prevent a slave owner from bringing one hundred slaves into a free state and setting up a plantation? Given the Court's decision in *Dred Scott*, could slavery be kept from spreading to the North? Lincoln worried that a follow-up case to *Dred Scott* would result in the Court declaring null and void all antislavery laws in the free states. In his "House Divided" speech, Lincoln stated, "We shall *lie down* pleasantly dreaming that the people of *Missouri* are on the verge of making their State *free;* and we shall *awake* to the *reality*, instead, that the *Supreme Court* has made *Illinois* a *slave* State."[11]

One antislavery Northerner, John Brown, had had enough. A veteran of the civil war in "Bleeding Kansas," Brown decided to make a bold strike against American slavery. In October 1859, after months of planning, Brown and a score of his supporters attempted to incite a slave rebellion.

His plan was to capture the federal munitions factories and warehouses in Harpers Ferry, Virginia, arm the slaves in nearby plantations, and encourage those slaves to start a revolt like the one that Nat Turner had attempted almost thirty years earlier. Brown failed. His revolt was crushed by federal troops, and Brown was found guilty of murder and treason and executed in December 1859. But Brown's act of insurrection spelled the end of compromise between North and South. War seemed inevitable.

Three days after Brown's death, while Congress was in session discussing Brown's aborted slave revolt, William Barksdale, a Mississippi congressman, attacked with a knife Thaddeus Stevens, an abolitionist Pennsylvania congressman. Lawmakers began going to work armed, ready for combat. Southerners began to speak openly about seceding from the Union. President James Buchanan attempted to hold together his fragmenting nation, but he was already a "lame duck" president completing his final year in office. He would pass the crisis to his successor, whom Americans would elect in November 1860.

The Election of Lincoln

The election of Lincoln in 1860 initiated the Civil War. Even before Lincoln took office, seven Southern states voted to withdraw from the Union. As Don E. Fehrenbacher states, "Talk of secession was almost as old as the Republic, but only in the 1850s did the idea crystallize into a definite movement for southern independence."[12] Southerners assumed that a Lincoln presidency and a Republican administration would pose an unacceptable threat to slavery; the South's response was secession.

In his First Inaugural Address, delivered on March 4, 1861, Lincoln attempted to assuage the South's fears. "I have no purpose, directly or indirectly, to interfere with the institution of slavery where it exists," Lincoln declared. "I believe I have no right to do so, and I have no inclination to do so." He also asserted that "in contemplation of universal law, and of the Constitution, the Union of these states is perpetual." He concluded his address by pleading with the South for reconciliation: "We are not enemies, but friends. We must not be enemies."[13]

But most Southerners did not see the Constitution and the Union as Lincoln saw them. To many Southerners the Union was not perpetual, and the Constitution was not a sacred contract; the Union was merely a club that its members could join and quit as they pleased. Many Southerners saw themselves as Virginians or Georgians or Alabamans first and as Americans second. But Lincoln was determined to use force, if necessary, to compel the rebellious South back into the Union. And so the war came.

A War for Union

When the war began in April 1861, it was not, in Lincoln's view, a war over slavery; it was a war to restore the Union. Lincoln's first public address on the war, delivered to Congress on July 4, 1861, comprises fifteen or twenty pages, but the words "slave" and "slavery" appear nowhere in the document. To Lincoln, the war was caused by an act of insurrection—the South's rejection of a lawfully elected presidential administration. In Lincoln's view, the war "presents the whole family of man, the question, whether a constitutional republic, or a democracy—a government of the people, by the people—can, or cannot, maintain its territorial integrity, against its own domestic foes."[14]

From the beginning of the war, however, abolitionists pushed Lincoln to make slavery a casualty of the war. Forcing the South back into the Union with slavery in place was foolish, in the view of many abolitionists, because surely another crisis would develop over slavery, and the South would simply secede again. A house divided on the issue of slavery could not stand. As the war continued, many Republicans came to believe that the war must serve two purposes: to reunite the fractured Union and to rid the nation forever of the institution that caused the fissure.

A War to End Slavery

Eventually Lincoln came to agree with those in the abolitionist wing of his party. On January 1, 1863, he signed the

Emancipation Proclamation, which freed the slaves in the states in revolt against the Union. At the same time, he urged the four slave states loyal to the Union to pass amendments to their constitutions outlawing slavery, and he prompted Congress to initiate the process of amending the United States Constitution to forbid slavery throughout the United States.

In November 1863, at Gettysburg, Pennsylvania, the scene of one of the battles that turned the tide of the war in the North's favor, Lincoln eloquently articulated the dual purpose of the war. He announced that the nation's Founding Fathers had established a nation "dedicated to the proposition that all men are created equal" and that the war was "testing whether that nation, or any nation so conceived and so dedicated, can long endure." He promised that through the crucible of war his nation would experience "a new birth of freedom" and that "government of the people, by the people, for the people, shall not perish from the earth."[15]

Resolving Fundamental Questions

The Civil War, which ended with the surrender of Confederate armies in 1865, resolved two fundamental questions that had troubled the American republic since its birth. First, it defined the meaning of Union. After the war, the United States was no longer a grouping of free and independent states, as the Declaration of Independence might have suggested; it was a nation, its unity perpetual. The South's secession and its quest for independence became known as the Lost Cause, an effort never again to be attempted. Second, the war resolved the issue of slavery. A nation dedicated to the proposition that all men are created equal could not tolerate slavery within its borders forever; slavery would have to die for the nation to achieve the lofty aims of its Founding Fathers. The Thirteenth Amendment to the United States Constitution, enacted in late 1865, prohibited slavery and involuntary servitude in all American states and territories.

The Civil War began a long process of uniting the divided American house. The unification process would be long and arduous. The war ruined the South's economy, and the effects of that destruction would be felt throughout the South for several decades. The slaves were free, but the South would impose legal, social, economic, and political restrictions on the freemen and their descendents that would remain in place for almost a century. When Lincoln stated, in his Second Inaugural Address, the need to "bind up the nation's wounds,"[16] he had probably not anticipated that the nation's wounds would take one hundred years to heal completely.

But the national unification process actually began when the rift between North and South seemed widest—in April 1861, when Confederate guns blasted away at Fort Sumter. As Civil War historian James M. McPherson points out, "Before 1861 the two words 'United States' were generally rendered as a plural noun: 'the United States *are* a republic.' The war marked a transition of the United States to a singular noun."[17] As a result of the Civil War, the United States *is* a republic, and that republic is slave-free.

Notes

1. Abraham Lincoln, *Selected Speeches and Writings*. New York: Vintage Books, 1992, p. 131.

2. Don E. Fehrenbacher, *Prelude to Greatness: Lincoln in the 1850s*. CA: Stanford University Press, 1962, p. 94.

3. Philip S. Foner, ed., *The Basic Writings of Thomas Jefferson*. Garden City, NY: Halcyon House, 1950, p, 24.

4. Bruce Catton, "Grant and Lee: A Study in Contrasts," in *The American Story: The Age of Exploration to the Age of the Atom*, ed. Earl Schenck Miers. Great Neck, NY: Channel Press, 1956, pp. 220–21.

5. Lincoln, pp. 111–12.

6. Quoted in Foner, p. 767.

7. Quoted in George M. Fredrickson, ed., *William Lloyd Garrison*. Englewood Cliffs, NJ: Prentice-Hall, 1968, p. 23.

8. Quoted in Mason Lawrence, ed., *Against Slavery: An Abolitionist Reader*. New York: Penguin Books, 2000, p. 119.

9. Henry David Thoreau, *Civil Disobedience and Other Essays*. New York: Dover Books, 1993, p. 23.

10. Quoted in Joan Hedrick, *Harriet Beecher Stowe: A Life*. New York: Oxford University Press, 1994. p 208.

11. Lincoln, p. 137.

12. Don E. Fehrenbacher, "Why the War Came," in *The Civil War: An Illustrated History*, by Geoffrey C. Ward, Ric Burns, and Ken Burns. New York: Alfred A. Knopf, 1990, pp. 85–86.

13. Lincoln, pp. 284, 286, 293.

14. Lincoln, p. 304.

15. Lincoln, p. 405.

16. Lincoln, p. 450.

17. James M. McPherson, *Battle Cry of Freedom: The Civil War Era*. New York: Oxford University Press, 1988, p. 859.

Chapter 1

A Nation Divides: The Causes of the Civil War

Turning|Points

IN WORLD HISTORY

The Causes of the Civil War: An Overview

Patrick Gerster and Nicholas Cords

In their book *Myth in American History*, Patrick Gerster and Nicholas Cords, history professors at Lakewood State Junior College, offer an overview of the scholarship on the causes of the Civil War. According to Gerster and Cords, some historians have allowed their regional loyalties to influence their assessments of the war's causes. After presenting a sampling of studies of the causes of the Civil War published between the late-nineteenth century and the mid-twentieth century, Gerster and Cords conclude that unresolved racial problems in the United States in the mid-nineteenth century were the key factor in igniting a war between the North and the South.

Humans find war endlessly fascinating. While warfare brings out the worst features of human nature, it also produces examples of heroism and self-sacrifice. And for Americans the Civil War, more than any other of the nation's conflicts, has drawn the greatest attention. The Civil War is *the* war as far as Americans are concerned and it seems to hold the key to the mysteries of the national experience. Why is this so? Because it was a conflict which pitted American against American. On the battlefields of Bull Run, Antietam, Vicksburg, and Chattanooga the future destiny of the nation was decided. The Civil War fundamentally tested both the American character and the strength of the nation's basic institutions. It sustained a national government and altered a developing national economy.

Having come to see that so much was at stake in the critical years from 1861 to 1865, both the American public and professional historians have never tired of studying, analyzing, and debating the meaning of the war. Books dealing with individual battles and the wartime exploits of such colorful individuals as Confederate General George Pickett and Union General John A. Logan roll from the presses each year. Magazines devoted to Civil War history continue to find popular appeal. Members of Civil War roundtables endlessly discuss the many engaging problems which the war offers both the trained professional and the history buff. Civil War battlefields still draw hundreds of thousands of vacationing Americans each year, many of whom have been said to feverishly purchase souvenirs inscribed "Made in Japan." The Civil War continues to have a deep effect both on the way that Americans behave and on their view of themselves as a people.

The process of myth development concerning the causes of the Civil War began shortly after the guns fell silent at Appomattox. And the first important expressions concerning causes were those written by men who thought they knew the situation well—they had either participated in the war directly or had solidly supported either the Union or the Confederate cause. But these were partisan points of view, and historical scholarship reinforced mythology. The Civil War seemed only to move from the battlefields to the pages of the history books. Professional historians in many cases became involved in a war of words as they allowed their regional loyalties to influence their histories.

The Views of Northern Historians

Northern historians, reflecting what now appears to have been a political-geographical bias, were quick to label the recent hostilities "The War of the Rebellion." They seemed less interested in telling an unbiased story of the war years than in trying to pin war guilt on the South. Making their case on behalf of the Union, the North's most accomplished historians—Francis Parkman, George Bancroft, and John L. Motley—all concluded that the Southern states had illegally seceded and were thus solely responsible for the conflict. In a manner reminiscent of treatment later accorded Germany during and after the First World War, these Yankee historians lent their prestige to the arguments on the cause of the war which most Northerners already accepted; that is, the South had been the enemy of continuing union and democracy.

The belief that a Southern conspiracy to establish a "slave empire" had caused the war seems now to have been based more on emotion than on fact. One finds, for example, that the service of Francis Parkman's brother in the Union army and his detention for a time as a prisoner of war by Confederate forces may have had something to do with Parkman's prejudice against the South. In addition, the idea of the Union took on such a sacred quality after the Civil War that it proved easy for many Americans to believe that Southern activities against the Union had been close to sacrilegious. Thus, some Northern historians were responding more to what the war symbolized than to what the evidence disclosed. They had a distinct picture of what the war should have meant to the nation before ever setting pen to paper. The pitched emotions of the war period were carried over into the histories. Historian Thomas Pressly has explained the psychology of these times particularly well:

> Just as the attack upon Pearl Harbor of December 7, 1941, served a later generation of Americans as a symbol of aggressive warfare, so did the Sumter episode serve the Unionists as a symbol of the belligerent confederacy in the very act of inaugurating unprovoked war . . . . In the wartime histories, as in the actuality of 1861, what gave meaning to Fort Sumter as symbol was the fact that the attack upon the fort was viewed as an assault upon the nation.

The skirmish at Fort Sumter, which was the first military confrontation between the warring sections, was not in a strict sense of course an "assault upon the nation" at all. The point was, however, that the North elected to take it to be just that. Myth was doing its part to emphasize certain facts at the expense of others. Needless to say, the nation's historical understanding of what had caused the war was to this point imperfect at best.

Influenced by a curious blend of nationalism and sectionalism (nationalism and Northern sectionalism had come to mean essentially the same thing) Northern historians continued to produce prejudiced writing on the causes of the Civil War until well into the 1880s. The unshakeable conclusion that the secession of the Southern states was in reality rebellion and treason continued to be the key concept with which Unionist historians both began and ended their studies. The former Union General John A. Logan, for example, carried on the tradition of the North's historical bias against the South in his book *The Great Conspiracy* (1886), which held Dixie responsible for the war by having supported slavery and the destruction of the Union, and—as Logan said—the "un-American doctrine of Free Trade." Given the biased viewpoints of these so-called bloody-shirt interpretations of the Civil War, it is little wonder that one had to look long and far for a Northern history of the war and the preceding period which did not drip with anti-Southern emotion and which was not therefore crudely mythical.

The Southern Historians' View

Not to be outdone in mythmaking, Southern historians in the decades after the Civil War clearly viewed the political and military crisis as a "War Between the States." In the South from 1861 to the 1880s, Confederate views on what had caused the Civil War dominated historical writing. Southerners seemed both unwilling and unable to see it as anything other than the South's Lost Cause. Historians such as Richmond journalist Edward A. Pollard (during the immediate postwar years at least) told the tale of civil conflict with a rebel yell. Even the moderate former vice-president of the Confederacy, Alexander H. Stephens, in *A Constitutional View of the Late War Between the States* (1868–1870), wrote history with a distinctly Southern bias. Thus it appeared that what the South had lost in the political arena and on the battlefield could somehow be regained through the verdict of history. One finds, for example, that the formation of the Southern Historical Society in 1869 by such prominent Confederates as R.M.T. Hunter, Jubal A. Early, and

Admiral Raphael Semmes was in the interest of "provid[ing] for the collection, preservation, and presentation to the world of materials which would vindicate Southern principles in the war." To attempt to answer the charges directed against their region by Northern historians, some Southerners took the classic position of arguing that the secessionist movement had not been a revolution at all. It was neither treasonous nor illegal. Rather, what the South had attempted to accomplish in the war was to preserve the integrity of the original Constitution. By trampling on the rights of the states and by not allowing for the protection of the South's legitimate political and economic interests, according to this Southern position, the North had violated the spirit if not the letter of the political guidelines set down for the nation in the Constitution. The establishment of the Confederate States of America, the argument went, was not an attempt to destroy existing American institutions and traditions. On the contrary, the South had reluctantly found war necessary in order to save the American way of life from Yankee political and economic aggression. In this sense, the North and not the South was responsible for causing the War Between the States.

The Inevitable Conflict

In the last years of the nineteenth century and into the early years of the twentieth, the emphasis on what had caused the Civil War began to change. Historians came to the conclusion that earlier explanations were unsatisfactory or incomplete and had reflected biased opinions. The residue of hatred left from the war was eroding, and the times seemed to call for an era of greater friendship between the sections. The idea that the Republicans were the party of union, the Democrats that of "Southern treason," which had enjoyed favor right after the war, for example, gradually passed from the political scene. So completely were attitudes changing in fact that Democrat Grover Cleveland was elected to the presidency in 1884—the first from his party to achieve the office since James Buchanan in 1856. It had taken nearly thirty years for the emotions of the war to cool. The reunion of the sections seemed nearly complete when Cleveland followed his election with the appointment of an ex-Confederate as a key cabinet official—General Lucius Quintus Cincinnatus Lamar, C.S.A., secretary of the interior.

The warmer relations between North and South which developed during this later era helped foster a new conclusion regarding Civil War guilt and causes; neither section was to blame, though the existence of slavery had been the principal cause. Both sections were innocent because slavery was a factor over which neither the North nor the South had much control. Historians concluded that the peculiar institution—not mortal human beings—had made the war inevitable, for it would have been impossible for Southerners or Northerners to have successfully dealt with the irrepressible forces which history and circumstance had set in motion. Americans, the argument went, had simply been swallowed up in a tidal wave of historical determinism. "Destiny," rather than individual Yankees or Confederates, had moved the nation almost against its will to cruelty, violence, and mass destruction. Conveniently, questions of guilt, accountability, and responsibility could be set aside. An illusion of "blamelessness" carried the day.

Indeed, both the general public and professional historians found these new views on the Civil War thoroughly acceptable. Each of the seven volumes that historian James Ford Rhodes published between 1893 and 1906, whose general title was *History of the United States from the Compromise of 1850*, endorsed this point of view and the work was greeted with both popular and critical acclaim. As the nation's major historical spokesman for this new understanding of the Civil War's origins, Rhodes was perhaps the key figure in offering Americans what they had come to believe and wanted to hear. Rhodes, of course, reflected the spirit of his times, and with his and other academic assistance Americans accepted the fiction that the nation's Civil War could be explained as a case where people had been trapped by history. The myth prevailed that they had been innocent and therefore guiltless victims of history's irrepressible forces.

In the 1920s, a shift in emphasis occurred while historians

continued to grapple with the problem of the "real" causes of the Civil War. Convinced, as earlier generations had been, that they were being completely impartial in their analysis, many now began to argue that the origins of the struggle between the Blue and the Gray could be explained in economic terms. This new "economic interpretation," set forth primarily by historian Charles Beard, became widely popular in its day as earlier views had been in theirs. Historians such as Beard could now explain the nation's past in terms of its economic development, having witnessed the great economic changes in America after Appomattox. America had moved from being a predominately rural and agricultural nation to one rapidly becoming urban and industrial. Publishing his views on the Civil War only two years before the beginning of the Great Depression of 1929, at the peak of 1920s "prosperity," it was logical that Beard would offer the explanation that the war had essentially been the capstone of a struggle between two conflicting economic systems—a capitalistic industrial North versus an aristocratic agricultural South. The economic point of view was as deterministic as the Rhodes conclusion regarding slavery, and this interpretation was not to satisfy everyone for all time.

The Repressible Conflict

Judging from the avalanche of writing which historians have loosed since Charles Beard presented his economic interpretation, it is clear that historians' quest for the elusive reality of the war's true beginnings continues. Convinced that history told only from an economic point of view was something less than complete, many historians came to feel that a revision of all earlier points of view on the causes of the war was in order. Indeed, by the 1940s almost every earlier view was under challenge from a group called the "revisionists."

In particular, revisionist historians questioned the idea held by economic historians and others that the war had been unavoidable or inevitable. Led by James G. Randall of the University of Illinois and Avery Craven of the University of Chicago, they argued instead that the war really had been a "needless" conflict. Reflecting the strong antiwar feelings in America during the 1930s, both concluded that, in a sense, war had come precisely *because* it lacked any fundamental "causes." According to Craven, for example, not even the existence of slavery in the South had created enough of a difference between the sections to make the war necessary. The war resulted from the numerous images, stereotypes, and myths which each section had created about the other. The highly charged emotional atmosphere created by radical secessionists and belligerent abolitionists helped produce feelings and misunderstandings which were for the most part irrational and unrealistic. If one were forced to identify *the* cause of the Civil War, Craven concluded, the explanation lay in the irrational mythology extremists on both sides had manufactured. James Randall's conclusions on the Civil War were similar to Craven's in that he also believed that the crisis resulted from "artificial" and "unreal" issues. His final emphasis was somewhat different from Craven's, however, in that he suggested that a "blundering generation" of politicians in union with a national psychology verging on the psychopathic were most responsible for the breakdown of what had been the United States.

Revisionism Revised

Predictably, the views of the revisionists have themselves been revised. Concerned that historians such as Craven and Randall had made too little of slavery as the institution and issue which had caused the Civil War, some historians have since come to argue the fundamental importance of the system of black bondage to the growth of hostile feelings between North and South. Whereas the revisionist historians had tended to focus their attention on the evil of war (writing as they did during the era of the 1930s and the Second World War), more recent historians, such as Arthur Schlesinger, Jr., in "The Causes of the Civil War: A Note on Historical Sentimentalism" (1949), have been inclined to emphasize the moral evils of slavery. Whereas earlier it seemed proper to condemn the nation for having allowed itself to degenerate into the immoral barbarism of war, historians now argued that the personal and economic exploitation of blacks was by far a greater corrupting influence on America. Questions of how the Civil War should have been avoided—which revisionists asked—completely miss the significant moral benefits which the war brought to the nation, according to this point of view. Only war could force the country to live up to its cherished ideals of human equality and freedom. Though war can seldom be condoned, in this instance it did have the effect of fulfilling America's faith. Despite such criticism, however, revisionism has had its positive effects in helping to clarify the nation's understanding of its Civil War. Revisionists did much to correct the errors, oversimplifications, and stereotypes created by earlier recorders of the historical record. In addition, they provided a solid platform upon which additional study into the causes of the Civil War could be built.

A final determination of the myth and the reality of the causes of the Civil War has, of course, still not been made. Each generation of historians must creatively select from the theories which previous scholars have offered, develop additional theories of their own, and attempt to move on to more complete and thorough explanations. The prejudiced views of early historians whose major efforts were essentially to justify the position of either the North or the South seem for the most part to have been rejected, but almost every other theory on the causes of the war appears to offer at least an element of truth. Beard's economic explanations of the war, for example, if viewed only by themselves offer at best an incomplete picture. It seems clear that humans are not driven to the point of war only by pocketbook considerations. Economic motives, however, do play a critical role in the affairs of nations. And even if it can be proven that the slave system of the South was as "capitalistic" as the industrial structure of the North—that the Yankee and the Cavalier were not distinct "types" economically—there is nonetheless much truth in the fact that the sections *believed* that they were different. In this way, most modern scholarship on the causes of the Civil War can accept the idea that both "the unrealities of passion" and "the failure of American leadership" were related in important ways to the myth that the North and the South had created conflicting cultures based on conflicting economies. Beard seemed to have fallen victim to the stereotypes of Cavalier and Yankee, yet the nation at large had also believed in them at the time of the Civil War and had at least to some degree based its conduct on a set of legendary beliefs similar to those with which Beard began his study.

A Final Analysis

In the final analysis, what historians have said about the causes of the Civil War vary widely. They have functioned as mythmakers in that they have too often offered far too simple explanations of a very complex era. Objectivity suffers and certain evidence is overlooked as historians read the predispositions and prejudices of their own generation into the past, and it is likely that similar charges will be lodged against scholars who today see slavery as the ultimate cause of the war—i.e., they reflect too much the civil rights consciousness of their age. All explanations of an event as historically important as the American Civil War are bound to be at least to some degree mythical. A total reconstruction of past reality is impossible, and it is equally impossible for a historian to divorce himself from his times. Keeping these caveats in mind it is understandable that, for the present generation at least, the significance of the Civil War lies not only with the political and economic problems created by slavery, but with the social problems of "race adjustment" as well. Thanks to the work of such historians as David Potter and Allan Nevins, one can see more clearly today than ever before that racial subordination of the black was the very root and essence of the American predicament of the mid-nineteenth century. Slavery, purely and simply, may not of itself have caused the Civil War, but slavery and the accompanying problem of the place of blacks in the affairs of the nation were the essential factors of American life upon which economic and political misunderstandings hinged. In attempting to explain these misunderstandings—both imagined and real—sometimes by overemphasis historians have created myths of their own. To emphasize one explanation of what caused the Civil War and to thereby exclude other explanations can only lead to the creation of myth. Understanding the many explanations offered by historians thus far would seem to offer the best hope of discriminating intelligently between myth and reality with respect to the coming of the Civil War.

Slavery Caused the Civil War

Don E. Fehrenbacher

Historian Don E. Fehrenbacher is the author of several books on Abraham Lincoln and the Civil War, including *Prelude to Greatness: Lincoln in the 1850s* and *Lincoln in Text and Context*. In this essay, included in *The Civil War: An Illustrated History* by Geoffrey C. Ward, Ric Burns, and Ken Burns, Fehrenbacher argues that the South's secession from the Union and the war that followed were caused by slavery. Southern states found the newly elected administration of Republican Abraham Lincoln a direct threat to slavery, and their response to that threat was secession from the Union. Within several weeks of Lincoln's election, even before he took office as president, Southern states led by South Carolina began to vote to withdraw from the Union. Ordinances of secession followed a decade during which the relationship between the North and South deteriorated due to disagreements over slavery.

Two weeks before Abraham Lincoln took the oath of office as President of the United States of America on March 4, 1861, Jefferson Davis was sworn in as President of a new republic that extended from South Carolina to Texas. Nothing in the history of the Civil War is more remarkable than the speed with which secession proceeded and the Confederacy took shape, once the outcome of the presidential contest was known. The rush to action reflected an intensity of feeling also expressed in much southern rhetoric. Political leaders, editors, and other spokesmen denounced the election of Lincoln as an outrage amounting virtually to a declaration of war on the slaveholding states. "Let the consequences be what they may," said an Atlanta newspaper, "whether the

Don E. Fehrenbacher, "Why the War Came," in *The Civil War: An Illustrated History*, edited by Geoffrey C. Ward, Ric Burns, and Ken Burns. New York: Alfred A. Knopf, 1990. Copyright © 1990 by Don E. Fehrenbacher. All rights reserved. Reproduced by permission of American Documentaries, Inc.

Potomac is crimsoned in human gore, and Pennsylvania Avenue is paved ten fathoms in depth with mangled bodies . . . the South will never submit to such humiliation and degradation as the inauguration of Abraham Lincoln."

Secession: A Crisis over Slavery

Why did the lawful election of a new President provoke such fury and lead so promptly to dissolution of the Union? First of all, no one at the time seems to have doubted that the secession crisis was a crisis over slavery. To be sure, there were other reasons for southern disaffection, such as a sense of having been reduced to economic vassalage by the commercial and industrial interests of the Northeast. Nevertheless, the grievances listed by the seceding states concentrated almost entirely on slavery. So did efforts in Congress to produce a compromise. So did the outpouring of public discussion. "The institution of African Slavery produced the Secession of the Cotton States," declared another Atlanta newspaper soon after Davis's inauguration. "If it had not existed, the Union of the States would, to-day, be complete." Lincoln had already said about the same thing in a letter to a southern leader: "You think slavery is *right* and ought to be extended; while we think it is *wrong* and ought to be restricted. That I suppose is the rub. It certainly is the only substantial difference between us."

The dynamic force at work in the crisis was southern perception of the Republican party, not merely as a political opposition, but as a hostile, revolutionary organization bent on total destruction of the slaveholding system. Fearful predictions filled the air. The Lincoln administration, it was said, would seek to repeal the fugitive-slave laws, abolish slavery in the territories and the District of Columbia, prohibit interstate trade in slaves, and reverse the Dred Scott decision through a reorganization of the Supreme Court. More than that, Republican control of the government would break down southern defenses against abolitionist propaganda and subject the slaveholding society to a mounting threat of internal disorder. The platform of the Republican party, according to an Alabama senator, was "as strong an incitement and invocation to servile insurrection, to murder, arson, and other crimes, as any to be found in abolition literature." Republicans must be dealt with as enemies, said a North Carolina newspaper; their policies would "put the torch to our dwellings and the knife to our throats."

Actually, Republican leaders were something considerably less than revolutionaries. Their party platform, which repudiated the kind of violence associated with John Brown and affirmed "the right of each state to order and control its own domestic institutions," did not have the ring of an incendiary document. Indeed, Republican antislavery doctrine amounted to a moral compromise with slavery that abolitionists were disposed to treat with scorn. Why, then, did so many southerners take an apocalyptic view of Lincoln's election? And on the other hand, why did so many northerners vote for Lincoln, knowing that his election would be disturbing to the peace of the nation? These are simple questions that soon lead one deep into historical complexities.

Sectional Discord Dates to the Founding of the Republic

Slavery had been a troublesome but marginal problem in the founding of the Republic and in national politics for three decades thereafter. Sectional discord in those years had been centered primarily on other public issues, such as the Hamiltonian financial program of the 1790s and the Jeffersonian Embargo of 1807. As late as 1832, it was federal tariff policy that provoked South Carolina's belligerent experiment in nullification. Furthermore, southerners of the early national period, if they defended slavery at all, had usually done so in qualified and contingent terms, portraying it as a regrettable legacy that was ineradicable in their own time, but not for all time. The Federal Constitution, while acknowledging the presence of slavery in the nation, seemed to treat it implicitly as an impermanent feature of American society. A generation imbued with the spirit of the Enlightenment found it easy to believe that the disturbing problem of human servitude would eventually yield to the benevolent forces of social progress.

Slaveholders Feel Threatened

By the middle decades of the nineteenth century, however, accumulating changes of great magnitude were dissolving such optimism and placing the American Union chronically at risk. The rise of the cotton kingdom had enhanced the value of slave labor and its importance in the national economy. Despite some northern efforts to restrict it, the slaveholding system had expanded westward as far as Missouri, Arkansas, and Texas. The nation's slave population tripled between 1800 and 1840. Yet, although slavery flourished, the slaveholding class suffered from a growing sense of insecurity as it came under fierce attack from a new breed of abolitionists and as the South settled ever deeper into the status of a minority section.

Slaveholders felt both physically threatened and morally degraded by the antislavery crusade. What they sought with increasing passion was not only security for their social system but vindication of their social respectability and personal honor. The defense of slavery accordingly lost its earlier strain of ambivalence and became more emphatic, with elaborate appeals to history, the scriptures, and racial theory. More and more, the South came to resemble a fortress under siege, expelling or silencing its own critics of slavery and barricading itself against abolitionist oratory and literature. Southerners in Congress closed ranks against even mild antislavery proposals, such as termination of slave trading in the District of Columbia. They argued that any concession to the spirit of abolitionism would denigrate the South and serve as an entering wedge for further attacks on the slaveholding system. During the final stages of the sectional controversy, many southern leaders compromised their own states' rights principles by demanding a Federal policy unreservedly protective of slavery. Some of them even insisted that all northern criticism of the institution must cease or be suppressed by the states in which it originated. One consequence of these and other proslavery excesses was the enlistment in the antislavery movement of a good many northerners who felt little sympathy for the slave but had developed a strong aversion to the "slave power."

From 1846 onward, the sectional issue that inflamed national politics was the status of slavery in the western territories. Apparently resolved by the Compromise of 1850, the problem arose again in a bitter struggle over Kansas, where for several years intermittent violence foreshadowed the great conflict that lay ahead. By the summer of 1858, it had become clear that Kansas would never be a slave state and that slavery was not taking root in any other territory. Yet the controversy grew in intensity, even as it seemed to be declining in relevance, perhaps because of a deepening awareness on both sides that the territories were just the skirmish line of a larger

Lincoln Identifies Slavery as the Cause of the Civil War

In his Second Inaugural Address, delivered about one month before the conclusion of the Civil War, President Abraham Lincoln identified slavery as the cause of the Civil War. According to Lincoln, American slavery was a serious national offense for which a just god sent upon the nation a terrible war.

One eighth of the whole population were colored slaves, not generally distributed over the Union, but localized in the Southern part of it. These slaves constituted a peculiar and powerful interest. All knew that this interest was, somehow, the cause of the war. To strengthen, perpetuate, and extend this interest was the object for which the insurgents would rend the Union, even by war; while the government claimed no right to do more than to restrict the territorial enlargement of it. . . . If we shall suppose that American Slavery is one of those offences which, in the providence of God, must needs come, but which, having continued through His appointed time, He now wills to remove, and that He gives to both North and South, this terrible war, as the woe due to those by whom the offence came, shall we discern therein any departure from those divine attributes which the believers in a Living God always ascribe to Him?

Abraham Lincoln, *Selected Speeches and Writings*. New York: Vintage Books, 1992, pp. 449–50.

conflict over the future of slavery and the regional balance of power in an expanding nation. Ever more ominously in this unremitting quarrel there loomed the threat of disunion.

Talk of Secession

Talk of secession was almost as old as the Republic, but only in the 1850s did the idea crystallize into a definite movement for southern independence. Until near the end of that decade, the out-and-out secessionists (or "fire-eaters") remained a relatively small group, except in South Carolina and one or two other states. But a much larger number of southerners were tempted by the idea and partly converted. They tended, for instance, to uphold the right of secession, while pondering its feasibility. Often they retained a strong attachment for the Union while at the same time yearning to cut loose from its antislavery elements. The election of Lincoln galvanized such men, and most of them were ready, when the time came, to be caught up in the excitement of establishing a new nation.

But secession, although it sprang from an impetuous spirit, was a complicated and highly formal enterprise, very difficult to set in motion. Earlier threats of disunion had nearly all arisen because of proceedings in Congress, which meant that a sectional crisis could always be defused by legislative compromise. In any case, the problem of slavery in the territories had ceased to be an urgent matter (except as it affected presidential politics within the Democratic party), and there was no other sectional issue with which Congress seemed likely to provoke a major crisis. Meanwhile, however, the South found itself facing a different kind of menace that might well become the trigger for disunion, and this was something over which Congress had no control—namely, the increasing possibility that antislavery forces would capture the presidency.

The Emergence of the Republican Party

Historians once explained the birth of the Republican party in rather simple terms as the response of outraged northerners to the Kansas-Nebraska Act of 1854, which opened up those two territories to slavery. Later scholarship indicates, however, that a fundamental realignment of the party system was already under way when the Kansas question arose. The change began at the local level and reflected concern about certain ethnocultural issues, such as nativism and temperance, to which the old parties seemed to be paying too little attention. Out of this local unrest there arose the Know-Nothing movement, organized politically as the American party, which for a time seemed likely to replace the failing Whig organization as the principal opposition to the Democrats. But the

Following the election of Abraham Lincoln, pictured above, as president, many Southern states withdrew from the Union because they believed slavery was threatened.

anti-Nebraska coalition of 1854, soon to take the name Republican, superimposed its political revolution upon that of the nativists and in the end absorbed much of the American party's membership. The emergence of Republicanism as a major political force was in fact a very complex event that cannot be attributed solely to antislavery zeal or to any other single cause. Nevertheless, what proved to be crucial in 1860 was not the true nature of the Republican party, whatever that may have been, but rather, southern perception of the party as a thinly disguised agency of abolitionist fanaticism.

For many southerners, the prospect of a Republican administration summoned up visions of a world in which slaveholding would be officially stigmatized as morally wrong, in which slaves would be encouraged to rise up against their masters, and in which national policy would move inexorably toward emancipation and racial equality. But to understand fully the reaction of the South to Lincoln's election, one must take into account not only the antislavery complexion of Republicanism but also the proslavery character of the Federal government before 1861. For nearly three-quarters of a century, southern slaveholders, along with northerners deferential to the slaveholding interest, had predominated in the presidency, the executive departments, the foreign service, the Supreme Court, the higher military echelons, and the Federal bureaucracy. Cabinet posts and other important positions were frequently entrusted to proslavery militants like John C. Calhoun, but no antislavery leader was appointed to high Federal office before Lincoln became President. The nation's foreign policy was conducted habitually and often emphatically in a manner protective of slavery. The presence of slaveholding in the national capital testified to its official respectability. In 1857, the Chief Justice of the United States awarded slavery a privileged status under the Constitution when he declared that the Federal government had no power to regulate the institution but did have "the power coupled with the duty of guarding and protecting the owner in his rights." When the secession crisis arose, James Buchanan, the Pennsylvania Democrat in the White House, blamed it entirely on "the incessant and violent agitation of the slavery question throughout the North." Is it any wonder that most southerners viewed the election of Lincoln as a revolutionary break with the past?

The danger of disunion apparently did not deter a great many persons from voting Republican in 1860. For one thing, the threat to secede had been heard so often that it was widely regarded as mere bluster, aimed at extracting concessions from fainthearted "Union-savers." Furthermore, many northerners persuaded themselves that the secessionists, even if serious, were just a noisy minority whose plot would be smothered by the stronger forces of southern unionism. The New York editor William Cullen Bryant spoke for perhaps a majority of Republicans when he remarked soon after the election: "As to disunion, nobody but silly people believe it will happen."

Cooperation or Secession?

Lending encouragement to such mistaken expectations was the amount of dissension in the South on the question of immediate withdrawal from the Union. Besides the many outright unionists, there were "cooperationists," who argued that secession should be preceded by a general southern convention, and there were conditional disunionists who wanted to wait until the Lincoln administration had committed an "overt act" of aggression against the South. But secessionist leaders knew that for their purposes delay was more dangerous than lack of full support. The shocking antislavery capture of the presidency provided a clear signal for disunion such as might never be sounded again, and its mobilizing effect would soon be wasted if action bogged down in debate. Cooperationist strategy had time and again proved unsuccessful. Therefore, the hour had come, said the fire-eaters, for secession to be undertaken in single file. One bold state must lead the way, drawing the rest of the South after it, state by state. As the movement proceeded, it would presumably gather momentum and eventually force even the border slave states to leave the Union.

When a South Carolina convention unanimously approved an ordinance of secession on December 20, 1860, it did so with full assurance that other states would follow. Sure enough, Mississippi seceded on January 9, 1861, then Florida and Alabama in the next two days, then Georgia, Louisiana, and finally Texas on February 1. At that point, however, the parade of departures came to a halt, as secession met defeat everywhere in the upper South. Later, of course, four more states seceded, but theirs was a different kind of decision that amounted to joining one side in a war already begun. The crucial determination to dissolve the Union in response to the election of Lincoln was made by just seven state governments, representing less than one-third of the free population of the entire South. Those same seven states of the lower South created the Confederacy, framed its constitution, and elected its President. Furthermore, it was men from the lower South who eventually made the fateful decision to open fire on Fort Sumter. Virginians, by way of contrast, lived for four years under a government that they had no part in establishing and fought for four years in a war that they had no part in initiating.

Driven by fear, anger, and pride into preemptive action against what appeared to be an intolerable future, the secessionist majorities in the lower South seized the initiative after Lincoln's election and forced a battery of hard choices on the rest of the country. The decisiveness of these men enabled them to shape the course of events to their liking for a time, although it served them badly at Fort Sumter. Their decisive behavior is the heart of the matter in any explanation of the outbreak of the Civil War, just as slavery is the heart of the matter in any explanation of that behavior.

Differing Geographic Conditions Intensified the Rift Between North and South

D.W. Meinig

D.W. Meinig, a professor of geography at Syracuse University, is the author of the three-volume study *The Shaping of America: A Geographical Perspective on 500 Years of History*, from which this selection is excerpted. Meinig suggests that the Civil War was caused by "a cluster of geographic conditions that impinged upon the developing crisis" between the North and the South during the 1850s. According to Meinig, slavery did not cause the war, but it was at the root of the conflict between the North and the South and magnified geographical differences between the two regions.

In one of his large and rich studies of America's great convulsion, Allan Nevins stated forthrightly: "It was a war over slavery *and* the future position of the Negro race in North America." Even as we acknowledge another historian's observation that "the academic controversy over the causes and character of the American Civil War seems as irreconcilable as the divergent viewpoints in the sectional controversy of the 1850s," it is impossible to avoid the basic truth—even if it is not of course the whole truth—of Nevins's assertion. The simplest test of the proposition is to try to imagine the irruption of such a massive conflict had there been no slavery and no presence of Blacks in something like their actual proportions and position within the American Union.

Nevins's statement does not assert a direct *cause*, and we should be wary of studies that purport to offer such an ex-

D.W. Meinig, *The Shaping of America: A Geographical Perspective on 500 Years of History, Volume 2: Continental America, 1800–1867*. New Haven, CT: Yale University Press, 1993.

planation; as [Don E.] Fehrenbacher warns: "What caused the Civil War is not a single historical problem but rather a whole cluster of problems, too numerous and complex to be incorporated into any single model of historical interpretation." Slavery did not cause the war, but it so permeated the issues that it must be seen as the root of the conflict. Our special geographic perspective leads to a similar kind of conclusion: although we may be certain that geography did not cause the war—and it must not be reified as an active force—it is just as certain that plausible interpretations of this vast drama must be grounded in a cluster of geographic conditions that impinged upon the developing crisis.

Geographic Conditions Caused a Rift Between North and South

1. *The United States was divided approximately equally into blocs of states forming two distinct kinds of territory, slave and free, within the one overall national structure.* It was the only such case extant. Brazil, the only other large national slave society, had no such internal partition. (The crucial difference between the United States and the common imperial pattern of a European state with slavery confined to overseas colonies was made clear in the 1830s when a home country parliament and administration imposed emancipation on their small, distant, and distinctly subordinate West Indian colonies.)

   a. The formal geographical boundary between the free and slave territories was defined very early along a clear east-west line across the entire breadth of the national territory.

   b. Huge territorial additions to the United States recurrently reopened the topic of extending this geographical line of separation. This issue provoked intense geopolitical disputes that were resolved by complex and ambiguous compromises, which proved unstable.

   c. There was no attempt to convert this internal boundary into a formal barrier, a patrolled line of controlled movement, or to inhibit in any way the free functioning of the general commercial and social systems of the nation, *except* for the movement of Blacks between these two sectors, as manumitted persons, as fugitive slaves, as repossessed slaves, or sometimes simply as free Blacks in routine jobs (as in attempts to prohibit Black sailors in Northern vessels from landing or having any contact with local Blacks, slave or free, in Charleston and other Southern harbors); and this exception was fraught with complications and controversy.

2. *The United States expanded westward along a broad front extending with equal vigor the populations and economies of its several sectors and preserving the initial North-South balance without disruptive strain.*

   a. Expansion was primarily a spread out of four regional societies of the Atlantic seaboard. The distinctive characteristics of these several societies were deep-rooted and not anchored on the simple presence or absence of slavery (which had been present in all during the colonial period). The result was a regional patterning of peoples and political cultures that expressed much more complex sets of interests and did not conform to the internal boundary between the slave and free halves of the nation.

   b. When the issue of the extension of slavery irrupted at the national level, concurrent initial expansion allowed new states to be admitted more or less as pairs, so that the sectional balance of senatorial representation was maintained into the 1850s.

3. *The North and the South were not primary regions of the United States.* They were made possible by the developing patterns of human geography, but they were created in part by conscious effort and took on shape and substance through the unfolding of events. Regional differences became magnified, narrowly focused, and essentially redefined through the agitations of dedicated ideologists.

   a. Abolitionists represented but one facet of moralistic political culture. Geographically this movement was almost entirely confined to Yankee and Quaker areas and in its more extreme forms represented only a small minority of such peoples.

b. Apologists of slavery as a positive form of modern society represented but one facet of a hegemonic political culture. Geographically this movement was most deeply rooted in South Carolina, largely confined to major plantation areas and probably supported by a relatively small minority of Southerners.

c. In the clash of the ideologies, selected regional differences became magnified into caricature, giving "a false clarity and simplicity," and undergirding the polarization in public perceptions (then and thereafter) of two distinct societies:

Yankee	Cavalier
industrial	agrarian
entrepreneurial	paternal
individualistic	familial
materialistic	organic
progressive	conservative

4. *The most critical, fundamental geographic feature was the distribution and proportion of Blacks within the total population of the South.* Because Blacks were a majority or large minority over so much of the region, Southern Whites assumed that any basic alteration in the legal and caste structure would destroy Southern society. Therefore, even those who regarded slavery as an evil (perhaps a majority) accepted it as an inherited burden that must be carried until White Southerners themselves found some way out.

a. No program for abolition or even gradual emancipation was considered feasible: colonization programs demonstrated the impossibility of large-scale deportations; to accept Blacks as local citizens would destroy White political dominance; to convert them into a peasantry would require a major redistribution of property; to transform them into wage-laborers would create an undisciplined and seasonally redundant body that would become an intolerable burden and threat to White communities.

b. The history of Santo Domingo and the presence of Black Haiti were a constant reminder of the terrifying possibility of Black revolt and revenge.

5. *The peculiar dual character of the United States, divided between areas of slavery and of nonslavery, was maintained by its federal structure.* Slaves defined as a species of property were under the jurisdiction of the individual states and not of the central government. When lagging population growth began to undermine the political power of the South, the weaker section feared that this interpretation of jurisdictions would be altered so as to threaten its vital interests. After the early failure of nullification, the South sought protection in drastic geopolitical alterations of the federal structure.

    a. Proposals for an internal restructuring of power, such as Calhoun's "concurrent majority" and Vallandigham's four-sections concept, failed to gain support.

    b. South Carolina's initiative in peaceful secession succeeded in creating a new seven-state confederation, but none of these actions was accepted as legitimate by the United States central government.

    c. The inherent geographic complication of federally garrisoned facilities within the bounds of seceding states was not resolved peacefully.

    d. Secession of states in the Upper South threatened to convert the long-standing slave-free interstate boundary into an international boundary. The central government was unwilling to accept that line of separation or any negotiated alternative line and undertook the task of forceful total reunification of the United States.

This very selective review makes no attempt to cover all the issues of this crisis. We are not searching for cause but only trying to illuminate certain geographical aspects. Wars are caused by human actions, by decisions, usually of very limited intent, whose results cannot be controlled or foreseen. Just as in the case of the American War of Independence, we can readily identify an incremental dynamic of action and reaction building from the local moves of small cadres of people (as at Fort Sumter) into a massive confrontation and convulsion.

Grant and Lee Represented Two Distinct Cultures

Bruce Catton

Bruce Catton, author of *Mr. Lincoln's Army*, *Grant Moves South*, *A Stillness at Appomattox*, and other studies of the Civil War, finds in generals Ulysses S. Grant and Robert E. Lee the key to the cultural differences between the North and the South during the mid-nineteenth century. These two military men "represented the strengths of two conflicting currents that, through them, had come into final collision." Lee represented the South's plantation aristocracy that resisted change, while Grant embodied a region characterized by rapid growth and change. Both regions, and both men, would be willing to fight a devastating civil war to protect their way of life.

When Ulysses S. Grant and Robert E. Lee met in the parlor of a modest house at Appomattox Court House, Virginia, on April 9, 1865, to work out the terms for the surrender of Lee's Army of Northern Virginia, a great chapter in American life came to a close, and a great new chapter began.

These men were bringing the Civil War to its virtual finish. To be sure, other armies had yet to surrender, and for a few days the fugitive Confederate government would struggle desperately and vainly, trying to find some way to go on living now that its chief support was gone. But in effect it was all over when Grant and Lee signed the papers. And the little room where they wrote out the terms was the scene of one of the poignant, dramatic contrasts in American history.

They were two strong men, these oddly different generals,

Bruce Catton, "Grant and Lee: A Study in Contrasts," *The American Story: The Age of Exploration to the Age of the Atom*, edited by Earl Schenck Miers. Great Neck, NY: Channel Press, 1956. Copyright © 1956 by Broadcast Music, Inc. Reproduced by permission.

and they represented the strengths of two conflicting currents that, through them, had come into final collision.

Lee Embodied the Aristocratic South

Back of Robert E. Lee was the notion that the old aristocratic concept might somehow survive and be dominant in American life.

Lee was tidewater Virginia, and in his background were family, culture, and tradition . . . the age of chivalry transplanted to a New World which was making its own legends and its own myths. He embodied a way of life that had come down through the age of knighthood and the English coun-

Robert E. Lee was seen by many as representing the South's plantation aristocracy and their resistance to change.

try squire. America was a land that was beginning all over again, dedicated to nothing much more complicated than the rather hazy belief that all men had equal rights, and should have an equal chance in the world. In such a land Lee stood for the feeling that it was somehow of advantage to human society to have a pronounced inequality in the social structure. There should be a leisure class, backed by ownership of land; in turn, society itself should be keyed to the land as the chief source of wealth and influence. It would bring forth (according to this ideal) a class of men with a strong sense of obligation to the community; men who lived not to gain advantage for themselves, but to meet the solemn obligations which had been laid on them by the very fact that they were privileged. From them the country would get its leadership; to them it could look for the higher values—of thought, of conduct, of personal deportment—to give it strength and virtue.

Lee embodied the noblest elements of this aristocratic ideal. Through him, the landed nobility justified itself. For four years, the Southern states had fought a desperate war to uphold the ideals for which Lee stood. In the end, it almost seemed as if the Confederacy fought for Lee; as if he himself was the Confederacy . . . the best thing that the way of life for which the Confederacy stood could ever have to offer. He had passed into legend before Appomattox. Thousands of tired, underfed, poorly clothed Confederate soldiers, long-since past the simple enthusiasm of the early days of the struggle, somehow considered Lee the symbol of everything for which they had been willing to die. But they could not quite put this feeling into words. If the Lost Cause, sanctified by so much heroism and so many deaths, had a living justification, its justification was General Lee.

Grant Embodied the Westerner

Grant, the son of a tanner on the Western frontier, was everything Lee was not. He had come up the hard way, and embodied nothing in particular except the eternal toughness and sinewy fiber of the men who grew up beyond the mountains. He was one of a body of men who owed reverence and obeisance to no one, who were self-reliant to a fault, who cared hardly anything for the past but who had a sharp eye for the future.

These frontier men were the precise opposites of the tidewater aristocrats. Back of them, in the great surge that had taken people over the Alleghenies and into the opening Western country, there was a deep, implicit dissatisfaction with a past that had settled into grooves. They stood for democracy, not from any reasoned conclusion about the proper ordering of human society, but simply because they

Ulysses S. Grant was often viewed as embodying the rapid growth and change of the North.

had grown up in the middle of democracy and knew how it worked. Their society might have privileges, but they would be privileges each man had won for himself. Forms and patterns meant nothing. No man was born to anything, except perhaps to a chance to show how far he could rise. Life was competition.

Yet along with this feeling had come a deep sense of belonging to a national community. The Westerner who developed a farm, opened a shop or set up in business as a trader, could hope to prosper only as his own community prospered—and his community ran from the Atlantic to the Pacific and from Canada down to Mexico. If the land was settled, with towns and highways and accessible markets, he could better himself. He saw his fate in terms of the nation's own destiny. As its horizons expanded, so did his. He had, in other words, an acute dollars-and-cents stake in the continued growth and development of his country.

Contrasting Cultures

And that, perhaps, is where the contrast between Grant and Lee becomes most striking. The Virginia aristocrat, inevitably, saw himself in relation to his own region. He lived in a static society which could endure almost anything except change. Instinctively, his first loyalty would go to the locality in which that society existed. He would fight to the limit of endurance to defend it, because in defending it he was defending everything that gave his own life its deepest meaning.

The Westerner, on the other hand, would fight with an equal tenacity for the broader concept of society. He fought so because everything he lived by was tied to growth, expansion, and a constantly widening horizon. What he lived by would survive or fall with the nation itself. He could not possibly stand by unmoved in the face of an attempt to destroy the Union. He would combat it with everything he had, because he could only see it as an effort to cut the ground out from under his feet.

So Grant and Lee were in complete contrast, representing two diametrically opposed elements in American life. Grant was the modern man emerging; beyond him, ready to come on the stage, was the great age of steel and machinery, of crowded cities and a restless, burgeoning vitality. Lee might have ridden down from the old age of chivalry, lance in hand, silken banner fluttering over his head. Each man was the perfect champion of his cause, drawing both his strengths and his weaknesses from the people he led.

Common Virtues

Yet it was not all contrast, after all. Different as they were—in background, in personality, in underlying aspiration—these two great soldiers had much in common. Under everything else, they were marvelous fighters. Furthermore, their fighting qualities were really very much alike.

Each man had, to begin with, the great virtue of utter tenacity and fidelity. Grant fought his way down the Mississippi Valley in spite of acute personal discouragement and profound military handicaps. Lee hung on in the trenches at Petersburg after hope itself had died. In each man there was an indomitable quality . . . the born fighter's refusal to give up as long as he can still remain on his feet and lift his two fists.

Daring and resourcefulness they had, too; the ability to think faster and move faster than the enemy. These were the qualities which gave Lee the dazzling campaigns of Second Manassas and Chancellorsville and won Vicksburg for Grant.

Lastly, and perhaps greatest of all, there was the ability, at the end, to turn quickly from war to peace once the fighting was over. Out of the way these two men behaved at Appomattox came the possibility of a peace of reconciliation. It was a possibility not wholly realized, in the years to come, but which did, in the end, help the two sections to become one nation again . . . after a war whose bitterness might have seemed to make such a reunion wholly impossible. No part of either man's life became him more than the part he played in their brief meeting in the McLean house at Appomattox. Their behavior there put all succeeding generations of Americans in their debt. Two great Americans, Grant and Lee—very different, yet under everything very much alike. Their encounter at Appomattox was one of the great moments of American history.

Early Battlefield Victories and the Prospect of European Intervention Fuel the South's Hope for Independence

Turning Points

IN WORLD HISTORY

President Jefferson Davis Developed a Grand Strategy for Winning the Civil War

Joseph L. Harsh

After the Southern states seceded from the Union and formed the Confederate States of America, the South's political and military leaders had to develop a strategy for repulsing any attempt by the North to force the rebellious states back into the Union. The South had the advantage of waging a defensive war because it did not have to conquer any Northern territory. According to Joseph L. Harsh, the author of *Confederate Tide Rising: Robert E. Lee and the Making of Southern Strategy*, Confederate president Jefferson Davis developed a sophisticated plan for military victory at the start of the Civil War. Rather than fight a strictly defensive war, Davis, according to Harsh, employed an "offensive-defensive" strategy that involved defending Southern territory from Northern invasion and launching offensive campaigns when opportunities for attack presented themselves. In Harsh's view, this strategy served the South well and "gave the Confederacy the best chance it would ever have to win its independence."

As in the case of military policy, it would be easy to conclude that the Confederacy lacked a grand strategy for winning the war. No leader ever committed to paper a comprehensive plan for coordinating Confederate military operations, and the inconsistencies in the employment of troops during the war could be seen as proof that Southerners possessed no controlling vision for the use of the impressive manpower they called into the field. On the one hand, some of the time the Confederates seemed to engage in a "perimeter defense" and attempt to contest every inch of Southern soil; a strategy that critics claim led to a fatal dispersal of force. On the other hand, Confederate armies launched several ambitious invasions of the North; a strategy that critics charge was bound to fail and frivolously squander scarce resources. In between extremes, Confederate commanders on the field so frequently preferred to attack rather than stand on the defensive that one pair of critics has suggested the influence of Celtic chromosomes.

In truth, the Confederacy did not possess a grand strategy in the modern sense of a highly detailed and unified program, nor even in the sense of the more primitive plans proposed by Winfield Scott and George McClellan for the North to restore the Union. Nonetheless, the Confederacy did evolve a grand strategy for victory. It can be found scattered throughout the words and actions of two men, a general who would not take center stage until after a year of the war had passed and the president of the Confederate States.

Davis Developed a Strategy for Victory

Jefferson Davis was an exceptionally strong war president. It could be argued that he shouldered a combined burden equal to that carried by George Washington and Abraham Lincoln. Davis had both to create a nation and its government out of whole cloth and at the same time fight a titanic struggle to determine its fate. Periodically, historians join in a survey to rank the presidents of the United States from best to worst. Judged by many of the criteria applied in this poll, if Davis were included, he ought to be ranked among the great and very near the top of the list.

During his four-year presidency, there was no doubt that Davis ran his administration, nor that he exerted considerable influence over the entire Confederate government. He was more active than most nineteenth-century presidents in submitting proposals for legislation, and, on the reverse side, he sent thirty-three veto messages to Congress. He was master of his cabinet and, although he did not always make happy choices, he was not so slow as some presidents to replace ineffective secretaries. He also set the framework and the tone for Confederate grand strategy.

Davis seldom put on paper specifics of strategy. He understood the impossibility of detailed control over the war at a distance from Richmond. Whether his insight derived from experiences in the Mexican War, his term as secretary of war during the 1850s, or simply from common sense, cannot be known. In any case, he recognized he would always be deficient in knowledge of geography and timely intelligence of troop dispositions. He acknowledged the need and with but few exceptions granted his commanders the "discretionary power which is essential to successful operations in the field." He aimed to select generals with the ability to design their own strategy and the willingness to accept the responsibility. As president, he labored to provide the men and the means and to protect his commanders from the ill-informed and contradictory crosscurrents of public opinion. He attempted—and usually succeeded—in confining himself to proposing "general purposes and views" for the guidance of his commanders.

Offensive Campaigns

Davis nonetheless did provide a firm strategic framework within which his generals in the field could work. Throughout most of the war, he expected them to undertake offensive campaigns whenever circumstances permitted. More than any other individual, Davis was responsible for the aggressive grand strategy of the Confederacy. Except for a brief hesitation in the winter of 1861–62, he operated on the belief that the South could only win the war by seizing and pressing the military initiative. He rejected the defensive because he understood the theoretical superiority of the offensive. "The advantage of selecting the time and place of attack was too apparent to have been overlooked," he proclaimed as early as March 1862. He also recognized that if the enemy were allowed to penetrate too deeply into the interior the "resources of our country will rapidly decline to insufficiency for the support of an army."

Davis believed the offensive grand strategy needed to be

applied in three distinct but related ways. First, in order to maintain territorial integrity, Confederate armies must aggressively foil enemy invasions. They must seize "the opportunity to cut some of his lines of communication, to break up his plan of campaign; and defeating some of his columns, to drive him from the soil . . . ." Second, offensive campaigns were required to claim the Confederacy irredenta. The president believed that Missouri and Kentucky belonged in the South and that Kentucky especially was essential to the viability of the new nation. He would also, at least on one occasion, enthusiastically support military intervention in Maryland.

Finally, and perhaps most controversially, Davis supported the idea known popularly as "carrying the war into Africa." Harking back to the Punic Wars, this term expressed the Roman belief that Carthage could not be defeated in Italy but only on its home ground in northern Africa. It also reflected the military thinking of the nineteenth century that "carrying the war into the heart of the enemy's country is the surest plan of making him share its

Confederate soldiers are pictured at Fort Gaines, Georgia, during the Civil War.

burdens and foiling his plans." It represented as well the views of a vocal segment of the Confederate citizenry who, once Southern soil had been violated, demanded vengeance be visited on the North.

Davis himself sought less to avenge the South than he did to weaken the North. From the start, he wanted the Northern people to feel the destructiveness of the war, and he sought to increase its cost to them and to sap their will. In June 1861, a month prior to the battle of First Bull Run, when Federals had gained no more than a toehold at Alexandria in northern Virginia, he lamented that lack of military preparedness compelled Southern troops to be "retiring from the Potomac," rather than "contending for the banks of the Susquehanna." Even at the depths of the black Confederate winter of 1861–62, he would deny that he had ever lapsed into a "purely defensive" strategy. Then, on the eve of the anniversary of First Bull Run, he would disparage any doubt "as to the advantage of invading over being invaded" by the enemy. "My early declared purpose and continued hope," he wrote to a critic, "was to feed upon the enemy and teach them the blessings of peace by making them feel in its most tangible form the evils of war." He insisted "the time and place for invasion has been a question not of will but of power." And in September 1862, when the possibility arose that Confederate armies might march into Pennsylvania and Ohio, he prepared a proclamation to be issued to the Northerners that declared the "sacred right of self-defense demands that, if such a war is to continue, its consequences shall fall on those who persist in their refusal to make peace."

Borrowing from Henri Jomini's War Strategies

After the war, Davis seemed to deny that the Confederacy had ever undertaken purely offensive military operations. As near as he would come to admitting this would be to confess that they had on occasion employed "offensive-defensive" operations, a phrase he borrowed, consciously or otherwise, from the Swiss military theorist Baron Henri Jomini. With this apparent circumlocution, Davis was able to maintain his claim that the Confederacy was the injured party engaged in a defensive war, and, when it went on the attack, it was simply following accepted military theory that the best defense is sometimes a good offense.

In truth, Davis gave away more of his argument than he may have realized by paraphrasing Jomini. The acknowledged interpreter of Napoleon did indeed provide the theoretical foundation for the Confederate grand strategy, but not in a way that furthered Davis's political rationale. In his most famous work, *Summary of the Art of War*, Jomini divided all wars into two simple categories according to a single aspect of their war aims. If a nation sought to conquer all or part of another, its war was offensive. If not, it was defensive. According to this broad—and not very helpful—definition, the Confederacy clearly engaged in a defensive war.

Logically, Jomini labeled any strategy for invasion and conquest an offensive strategy. With less logic and with confusing consequences, he called any strategy that did not aim at invasion and conquest a defensive strategy. He then proceeded to subdivide defensive strategies into alternative and substantially different categories. He described the first option as the "passive defense," an updated version of the strategy of delay employed by Roman General Fabius Cunctator against the military genius of Hannibal of Carthage. In the passive defense a general attempted to frustrate his opponent with feints and minor engagements, bait him into exhausting pursuit far away from the enemy's base of supplies, all the while avoiding pitched battles. In principle Jomini opposed the passive defense because he believed that only initiative—when correctly applied—could win wars. He advised against the use of this first strategy unless a nation were hopelessly outnumbered or outgeneralled.

Jomini believed the best course open to a nation engaged in a war not aimed at conquest was the "active defense" or—as he unhappily insisted on calling it at times—the "defensive-offensive." Herein, the general, even though he operated within a defensive political framework, seized the initiative to defeat the enemy, either by maneuvers that forced the enemy army to retreat or by combat that destroyed it. Jomini believed the side that maintained and pressed the initiative would eventually win, while the side that merely reacted would inevitably lose.

Whether consciously or coincidentally, Jefferson Davis's thinking ran parallel to Jomini's theories. In political terms, Davis needed to argue to the world that the Confederacy fought only in its own self-defense. But, in the military realm, he believed he must adopt the offensive, the only grand strategy that would lead to victory. Where Davis and the Confederates stretched Jomini's theory—if indeed they did not exceed it—was by including invasion as appropriate in their conduct of a defensive war.

Davis's term, the "offensive-defensive," may well be adopted to designate Confederate grand strategy, but it must be understood that offensive was much the greater element in the alloy. From the attack on Fort Sumter in April 1861 to the assault on Fort Stedman in March 1865, the Confederates consistently—albeit not invariably—used the offensive, on both the strategic and tactical level, to try to gain their war aims. It is especially appropriate to note, as a prelude to Lee's campaign in September 1862, that it was the Confederates who first set foot across the Potomac. In May 1861 they seized Maryland Heights opposite Harpers Ferry three weeks before the Federals occupied Alexandria and Arlington Heights.

Three Phases of the War

Although obscured by the telescoping effect of history, the first eighteen months of the war divided into three distinct and drastically different phases for the Confederacy. In the opening six months, from April to October 1861, the Confederates pursued a straightforward program for asserting control over the border states and territories. Southern armies achieved a string of stunning successes that carried their standards far toward their final intended boundaries.

A disastrous six-month period followed, from November through April 1862, in which the Confederates relied upon a largely defensive posture to hold onto their gains. In this second phase, the Confederacy suffered a staggering reversal of fate that plunged its citizens into despair and raised

considerable doubts over its ultimate ability to win independence. By the anniversary of the fall of Sumter, the brief experiment with a strategy of defense had nearly lost the war
for the South.

The third phase opened in April and May of 1862 and
witnessed the Confederacy's most determined attempt to
mobilize its manpower, concentrate its armies, and press forward with the offensive. Coincident with the start of this
third phase there appeared at the right time and place the
second central figure in Confederate grand strategy. Robert
E. Lee assumed command of the army in Virginia, and during the summer that followed he put flesh onto Jefferson
Davis's framework for the offensive. Lee's strategy to de-
moralize the North and, for the most part, his execution of
that strategy gave the Confederacy the best chance it would
ever have to win its independence.

Victory at Bull Run Sustains the Confederate Cause

Geoffrey C. Ward, Ric Burns, and Ken Burns

The American historian Geoffrey C. Ward and filmmakers Ken and Ric Burns collaborated on *The Civil War*, an award-winning documentary film, and *The Civil War: An Illustrated History*, a text to accompany the film. This excerpt from their book documents the euphoria in the South and the dejection in the North following the convincing Confederate victory at the Battle of Bull Run, the first major battle of the Civil War and the first of two major battles fought near Manassas, Virginia. In the South, the engagement became known as the Battle of First Manassas. The battle featured a fierce Federal offensive and a staunch Confederate defense, followed by a Rebel counterattack that sent Yankee troops scrambling back toward Washington. The North's first invasion of Southern soil resulted in a devastating military and psychological defeat for the Union.

On July 18, [1861] the volunteer Union army, 37,000 strong, marched south into Virginia. A reporter for the Washington *Star* described the spectacle:

> The scene from the hills was grand . . . regiment after regiment was seen coming along the road and across the Long Bridge, their arms gleaming in the sun. . . . Cheer after cheer was heard as regiment greeted regiment, and this with the martial music and sharp clear orders of commanding officers, made a combination of sounds very pleasant to the ear of a Union man.

Geoffrey C. Ward, Ric Burns, and Ken Burns, *The Civil War: An Illustrated History*. New York: Alfred A. Knopf, 1990. Copyright © 1990 by American Documentaries, Inc. All rights reserved. Reproduced by permission of American Documentaries, Inc.

The northern troops had a good time despite the fierce heat. "They stopped every moment to pick blackberries or get water," General [Irvin] McDowell remembered, "they would not keep in the ranks, order as much as you pleased. . . . They were not used to denying themselves much; they were not used to journeys on foot." It took them two and a half days to march twenty-five miles, a stretch seasoned troops would routinely cover in half the time later in the war.

Elisha Rhodes had a good time, too. "Our regiment stacked arms in a large meadow," he wrote. "Rail fences were plenty and we soon had fires burning and coffee cooking in our cups. . . . I enjoyed the evening by the fire and speculating on what might happen on the morrow."

A Grand Spectacle

Hundreds of Washington civilians rode out to join the advancing army, hoping to see a real battle. Some brought binoculars, picnic baskets, bottles of champagne. "The French cooks and hotel-keepers," William Howard Russell wrote, "by some occult process of reasoning, have arrived at the conclusion that they must treble the prices of their wines and of the hampers of provisions which the Washington people are ordering to comfort themselves at their bloody derby."

Some of the troops rather liked the notion of fighting their first battle in front of illustrious spectators. "We saw carriages and barouches which contained civilians who had driven out from Washington to witness the operations," a Massachusetts volunteer remembered. "A Connecticut boy said, 'There's our Senator!' and some of our men recognized . . . other members of Congress. . . . We thought it wasn't a bad idea to have the great men from Washington come out to see us thrash the Rebs."

[Confederate General P.G.T.] Beauregard knew the northerners were coming. Mrs. Rose O'Neal Greenhow, a prominent society leader in Washington and the aunt of [Senator] Stephen A. Douglas, was one of those who had seen to that, sending him word of the advance, her coded note concealed in the hair of a sympathetic southern girl. And he had ordered his men to form a meandering eight-mile line along one side of Bull Run Creek near a railroad center called Manassas Junction.

McDowell Attacks

McDowell moved first on Sunday morning, July 21, sending his men across the creek a little after nine. An onlooker remembered that the advancing Union army looked like "a bristling monster lifting himself by a slow, wavy motion up the laborious ascent."

Elisha Rhodes recalled the first serious shooting he ever heard:

> On reaching a clearing separated from our left flank by a rail fence, we were saluted by a volley of musketry, which, however, was fired so high that all the bullets went over our heads. . . . My first sensation was . . . astonishment at the peculiar *whir* of the bullets, and that the Regiment immediately laid down without waiting for orders. Colonel Slocum gave the command: "By the left flank—MARCH" and we commenced crossing the field. One of our boys by the name of Webb fell off the fence and broke his bayonet. This caused some amusement, for even at this time we did not realize that we were about to engage in battle.

The Battle of Bull Run, depicted above, was the first major battle of the Civil War, and resulted in a devastating defeat for the Union.

Not far away, Union cavalrymen, wearing crisp new uniforms and waiting to be ordered to the front, tried not to look as the first bloody, wounded men were carried past them to a surgeon's tent. Some, who failed to avert their gaze fast enough, vomited from their saddles.

Union Troops Gain the Advantage

Still, at first it all seemed to be going just as McDowell had planned. His divisions tore at the Confederate left and began to turn it, driving the rebels from one position after another. "We . . . fired a volley," a Massachusetts private wrote, "and saw the Rebels running. . . . The boys were saying constantly, in great glee, 'We've whipped them.' 'We'll hang Jeff Davis to a sour apple tree.' 'They are running.' 'The war is over.'"

On a green hillside three miles away, civilian onlookers waved their hats and fluttered their handkerchiefs. It was not yet noon.

"General McDowell rode up," a Union lieutenant recalled, "dressed in full uniform, including white gloves, and told us we had won a great victory. . . . We cheered him vociferously and felt like veritable heroes."

Northern victory seemed so sure, an officer remembered, that on one part of the battlefield some of the Union men stopped to gather souvenirs among the rebel troops who had fallen on the slope.

> What a horrible sight it was! Here a man, grasping his musket firmly in his hands, stone dead; several with distorted features, all horribly dirty. Many were terribly wounded, some with legs shot off; others with arms gone. . . . So badly wounded they could not drag themselves away . . . slowly bleeding to death. We stopped many times to give some a drink and soon saw enough to satisfy us with the horrors of war, and so, picking up some swords and bayonets, we . . . retraced our steps.

General Stonewall Jackson Rallies the Confederates

But holding a hill at the center of the southern line was a Virginia brigade commanded by Thomas J. Jackson, who be-

President Jefferson Davis Voices the South's Optimism

In a message to the Confederate Congress delivered on November 18, 1861, Jefferson Davis, president of the Confederate States of America, voiced the optimism felt throughout the entire South in the early months of the war. Davis's confident tone resulted from Confederate battlefield victories during the first six months of the war.

When the war commenced the enemy were possessed of certain strategic points and strong places within the Confederate States. They greatly exceeded us in numbers, in available resources, and in the supplies necessary for war. Military establishments had been long organized and were complete; the Navy, and for the most part the Army, once common to both, were in their possession. To meet all this we had to create not only an Army in the face of war itself, but also the military establishments necessary to equip and place it in the field. It ought indeed to be a subject of gratulation that the spirit of the volunteers and the patriotism of the people have enabled us, under Providence, to grapple successfully with these difficulties. A succession of glorious victories at Bethel, Bull Run, Manassas, Springfield, Lexington, Leesburg, and Belmont has checked the wicked invasion which greed of grain and unhallowed lust of power brought upon our soil. . . . After more than seven months of war the enemy have not only failed to extend their occupancy of our soil, but new States and Territories have been added to the Confederacy, while, instead of their threatened march of unchecked conquest, they have been driven, at more than one point, to assume the defensive, and, upon a fair comparison between the two belligerents as to men, military means, and financial condition, the Confederate States are relatively much stronger now than when the struggle commenced.

Dunbar Rowland, *Jefferson Davis: Constitutionalist, His Letters, Papers and Speeches.* Jackson: Mississippi Department of Archives and History, 1923, p. 167.

lieved the southern cause literally sacred and was able to convey that religious certitude to his men. While other southern commands wavered, his held firm. General Bernard Bee of South Carolina, trying to rally his own frightened men early that afternoon, shouted, "Look, there is Jackson with his Virginians, standing like a stone wall!" Bee himself was killed a little later, but the rebel lines held and the nickname stuck.

It was the turning point. The fighting seesawed back and forth across the hillside from two to four in the afternoon. Between the armies stood a farmhouse, the home of Judith Henry, an elderly widow too ill to move. Union shells ripped through the wall of her bedroom, tearing off the old woman's foot and riddling her body.

Confederate reinforcements began to arrive, led by General Joseph E. Johnston, who had now found it within him to draw his sword against his old flag. The first came on horseback, led by Colonel Jubal Early. Many more arrived by train, something new in war.

The Union men, most of whom had now been marching and fighting in brutal heat without food or water for fourteen hours, were demoralized to see fresh rebels pouring onto the field. "Where are *our* reserves?" some were heard to ask.

A Confederate Counterattack

At about four, Beauregard ordered a massive counterattack. Jackson urged his men to "yell like furies!" The high-pitched rebel yell first heard that afternoon—half exultant shout, half foxhound's yelp—would eventually echo from a thousand battlefields. "There is nothing like it this side of the infernal region," a Union veteran remembered many years after the war. "The peculiar corkscrew sensation that it sends down your backbone under these circumstances can never be told. You have to feel it, and if you say you did not feel it, and heard the yell, you have *never* been there."

To Beauregard's delight, the northerners began to edge backward. "I dispatched orders to go forward in a common charge," he recalled. "Before the full advance of the Confederate ranks the enemy's whole line irretrievably broke, fleeing across Bull Run by every available direction."

A Union Retreat

The retreat became a rout, McDowell admitted, "and this degenerated still further into a panic." Frightened civilians and frightened soldiers alike pushed and shoved to get away from the battlefield. "They plunged through Bull Run wherever they came to it," a rebel officer wrote, "regardless of fords or bridges, and there many were drowned. . . . We found . . . along the road, parasols and dainty shawls lost in their flight by the frail, fair ones who had seats in most of the carriages of this excursion."

Albert G. Riddle, an Ohio congressman, and two or three of his colleagues tried to turn the soldiers back.

> We called to them, tried to tell them there was no danger, called them to stop, implored them to stand. We called them cowards, denounced them in the most offensive terms, put out our heavy revolvers and threatened to shoot them, but all in vain; a cruel, crazy, mad, hopeless panic possessed them, and communicated to everybody about in front and rear. The heat was awful, although it was now about six; the men were exhausted—their mouths gaped, their lips cracked and blackened with the powder of the cartridges they had bitten off in the battle, their eyes starting in frenzy; no mortal ever saw such a mass of ghastly wretches.

Elisha Rhodes found himself among those demoralized men.

> I . . . struggled on, clinging to my gun and cartridge box. Many times I sat down in the mud determined to go no further, and willing to die to end my misery. But soon a friend would pass and urge me to make another effort, and I would stagger a mile further. At daylight we could see the spires of Washington, and a welcome sight it was. . . . The loss of the regiment in this disastrous affair was ninety three killed, wounded or missing.

The Union army remembered it as "the great skedaddle."

No one knows what might have happened had the southern army pursued them. "A friend in the federal capital," Mary Chesnut noted later, "writes me that we might have walked into Washington any day for a week after Manassas, such was the consternation and confusion there." But in fact the southern army was nearly as unprepared for its victory as its foes had been for their defeat, and a heavy downpour the next morning turned the roads to mud and made the question academic.

The Confederates discovered Congressman Albert Ely of New York hiding behind a tree and carried him off to Richmond. "The Yankee Congressman came down to see the fun," one rebel soldier said, "came out for wool and got shorn." President Davis himself sent the distinguished prisoner a pair of blankets to demonstrate to his people how southern gentlemen treated those whom they had defeated in battle.

A Great Confederate Victory

Davis, who had ridden out to see the fighting for himself, was jubilant. "Your little army," he told his people, "derided for its want of arms, derided for its lack of all the essential material of war, has met the grand army of the enemy, routed it at every point, and it now flies, inglorious in retreat before our victorious columns. We have taught them a lesson in their invasion of the sacred soil of Virginia."

Manassas had been *"one of the decisive battles of the world,"* wrote a prominent Georgia secessionist. It "has secured our independence." Persuaded that they had already won the war, that the North would now have no choice but to sue for peace, some Confederate volunteers left the army, eager to get home for the autumn harvest.

Sam Watkins, who arrived with his Tennesseans at Manassas Junction after the shooting had stopped, recalled the letdown he and his friends felt:

> We felt that the war was over, and that we would have to return home without even seeing a Yankee soldier. Ah, how we envied those that were wounded. We . . . would have given a thousand dollars . . . to have had our arm shot off, so we could have returned home with an empty sleeve. But the battle was over and we left out.

Some 4,500 men were killed, wounded, or captured on

both sides in the battle that the North called Bull Run and the South remembered as Manassas.

Disillusion in the North

William Howard Russell watched the northern army stagger back into Washington.

> I saw a steady stream of men, covered with mud, soaked through with rain, who were pouring irregularly . . . up Pennsylvania Avenue toward the Capitol. A dense stream of vapor rose from the multitude; but looking closely . . . I perceived they belonged to different regiments, New Yorkers, Michiganders, Rhode Islanders, Massachusettsers, Minnesotians, mingled pell-mell together.

Russell asked one pale young man who "looked exhausted to death" whether the whole army had been defeated. "That's more than I know," the soldier answered. "I know I'm going home. I've had enough fighting to last my lifetime."

"Today will be known as BLACK MONDAY," wrote George Templeton Strong when the bad news reached New York. "We are utterly and disgracefully routed, beaten, whipped by secessionists."

[Newspaper editor] Horace Greeley, who had urged [President] Lincoln to launch the premature drive on Richmond that had resulted in the defeat at Bull Run, now demanded that the President consider abandoning the entire struggle for the Union: "On every brow sits sullen, scorching, black despair . . ." he wrote. "If it is best for the country and for mankind that we make peace with the rebels, and on their own terms, do not shrink even from that."

A Second Victory at Bull Run Offers the Prospect of European Intervention on Behalf of the South

Howard Jones

Through the first two years of the Civil War, the South hoped that European powers such as Great Britain and France might intervene in the conflict on its behalf or at least recognize the Confederate States of America as an independent nation. At the start of the war, President Abraham Lincoln imposed a blockade of Southern ports, severely limiting the export of the South's cotton to Europe. The Confederacy hoped that Great Britain or France might break the blockade to reopen trade with the South. The Confederacy realized that it would need battlefield victories to convince Europe of its legitimacy, and a convincing Confederate victory at the Second Battle of Bull Run in late August 1862 brought the South close to its goal of obtaining recognition from France and Great Britain. In this excerpt from his book *Abraham Lincoln and a New Birth of Freedom*, Howard Jones, the chair of the department of history at the University of Alabama, discusses the French and British moves toward intervention after the South's second victory at Bull Run.

Intervention became even more likely in mid-September 1862, when news arrived in Europe of the Union's second resounding defeat at Bull Run. Confederate armies under Gen. Robert E. Lee repelled the Union forces and prepared to take the war north—into Union territory. The elder Adams in

London sank into despondency. He could not have known that matters were even worse than they appeared. The Union's leaders in Washington had learned that General McClellan had stood idly nearby with his forces during the battle, refusing to help the entrapped fellow soldiers falling in droves before the deadly Confederate assault. [Secretary of War Edwin] Stanton and [Secretary of Treasury] Chase led other irate cabinet members in demanding that the president remove McClellan from command. Attorney General Edward Bates warned Lincoln of the imminent fall of the nation's capital. The president, according to Bates, "seemed wrung by the bitterest anguish," even stammering that he was "almost ready to hang himself." But he refused to relieve McClellan, declaring that "he excels in making others ready to fight."

European Intervention

The Union's second disaster at Bull Run seemed to make European intervention nearly inescapable. [British foreign secretary] Russell triumphantly assured [British prime minister] Palmerston that McClellan's failure to deliver on his promise to conquer the South gave further justification for a British intervention. Indeed, the foreign secretary had become an earnest advocate of recognition. He asked [French foreign minister] Thouvenel about a joint suggestion of an armistice that, if rejected, would lead to British, French, Austrian, Prussian, and Italian recognition of the South as "Independent Confederate States." Such a drastic measure might "dispose the North to Peace."

Both Mercier's dispatches and numerous press stories had reached Thouvenel by early September, confirming in his mind the hopelessness of northern efforts to subjugate the South. The foreign secretary conveyed these thoughts to [Union minister in Paris William] Dayton but in a sympathetic fashion. The North should have let the South go at the outset of the sectional conflict, Thouvenel declared. In a year or so, he insisted, those states would have returned to the Union, albeit with suitable safeguards for slavery and states'-rights principles. But the Union's resort to force drastically changed the situation. "I think that the undertaking of conquering the South is almost superhuman . . . [and] to me the undertaking seems impossible." Thouvenel agreed with the British that the North was incapable of subjugating a region so large and a people so numerous.

Thouvenel clearly had in mind a foreign mediation of the war. Russell's interest in the project was undeniable, as indicated by the British ambassador in Paris. In conversation with Thouvenel, Lord Cowley had suggested an armistice that, if rejected, would lead to a threat to recognize the South. Thouvenel remained dubious about the chances of the Union's accepting such an intervention. And yet he wanted the war to end before the cotton shortages caused irreparable damage to the French textile industry, and he desperately desired a postwar America strong enough to balance British maritime interests. Perhaps, Thouvenel almost wistfully wrote [French minister Henri] Mercier, Second Bull Run had finally convinced northerners to call off the war.

The Union's Resolve

But as was the case following the Union's first defeat at Bull Run in July 1861, the British and French erroneously expected the Union to admit to the futility of the war. Both times the European powers felt confident that the Union would come to its senses about the impossibility of subjugating the South; both times they were sorely disappointed. Instead of accepting southern separation, the Union rallied its soldiers to carry on the fight. Although fate had seemingly dealt a final, climactic blow at Second Bull Run (had not [British ambassador William] Stuart earlier assured London that only "another Bull Run" would convince the North to stop fighting?), it had instead injected an uplifting sense of martyrdom into the Union's cause—particularly as Lincoln increasingly raised his voice against slavery in an attempt to define the struggle as one of righteousness versus evil. Only through long-suffering and torment, he realized, could great changes take place in a society so set against change. Even while Russell and Thouvenel expressed the feelings of their people in denying the possibility of a Union

victory, the Lincoln administration baffled and infuriated
Europeans by speaking glowingly of inevitable triumph and
hardening its resolve against foreign intervention.

Mercier perhaps grasped the intensity of Union feeling
when he talked with [Secretary of State William] Seward
about European intervention in the aftermath of Second
Bull Run. The French minister first suggested mediation.
Was not the secretary of state aware of the heightened foreign interest in ending the war? "I have noticed it," Seward
roughly responded, "but as for us it would be a great mis-
fortune if the powers should wish to intervene in our affairs." Mediation presupposed a disposition by the Union to
make concessions that admitted to the legality of secession.
"There is no possible compromise, tell Mr. Thouvenel, and
at any price, we will not admit the division of the Union." In
a hard-fought effort to reciprocate Mercier's assurances of
goodwill, Seward grimly declared that "we do not doubt
your sentiments but the best testimony that you are able to
give us of it is that you will stay out of our affairs." The only
feasible solution short of prolonged war, Mercier inter-
jected, was to establish two "confederated Confederacies."
But Seward abruptly cut off this line of thought by reem-
phasizing the impossibility of southern separation from the
Union. "Do not believe for a moment," he exclaimed with
mounting exasperation, "that either the Federal Congress,
myself or any person connected with this government will in
any case entertain any proposition or suggestion or arrangement or accommodation or adjustment from within or without upon the basis of a surrender of the Federal Union." Not
until the South surrendered would the North cease to fight.

In a bitter twist of fate, the British and French had become
more determined to intervene in the war just as the Union
became even more determined to prevent that disaster. Mediation, armistice, recognition—no form of foreign intervention appealed to the Union because the measure automatically bestowed, at the minimum, de facto nationhood status
to the South. Emancipation, assumed by the Union to be the
most decisive step intended to thwart that intervention, took
on the appearance overseas of a maniacal effort to incite a

slave insurrection conducive to a race war and now emerged, almost paradoxically, as an essential element in the European powers' deliberations for a direct involvement. Idealistic and realistic considerations had combined in separate and independent processes on both sides of the Atlantic to promote a foreign intervention that could profit only the South.

Other Repercussions of the South's Victory at Bull Run

The Union's defeat at Second Bull Run had both national and international repercussions. On the domestic front, Confederate forces under [General Robert E.] Lee turned northward, wishing to take the war out of the South and perhaps deliver a knockout blow. The drive north might even persuade foreign powers to recognize the Confederacy. Indeed, the British became even more certain that southern independence was a fact that only the stubborn North refused to accept. The time had come to end the fighting on the basis of a separation, or so many British observers argued in the autumn of 1862. The *Times* and the *Morning Post*, both more often than not expressing the views of the Palmerston ministry, urged recognition of the South, whereas the London *Morning Herald* captured the feelings of many readers by making a broad humanitarian appeal: "Let us do something, as we are Christian men." Whether "arbitration, intervention, diplomatic action, recognition of the South, remonstrance with the North, friendly interference or forcible pressure of some sort . . . let us do something to stop this carnage."

The popular clamor resulting from Second Bull Run appeared to be the last necessary ingredient in convincing the Palmerston ministry to intervene. The prime minister exulted in the news from abroad. "The Federals," he declared to Russell, "got a very complete smashing, and it seems not altogether unlikely that still greater disasters await them, and that even Washington or Baltimore may fall into the hands of the Confederates. If this should happen," he added with growing conviction, "would it not be time for us to consider whether . . . England and France might not address the contending parties and recommend an arrangement upon the basis of separation?" If either North or South rejected a mediation offer, England and France should "acknowledge the independence of the South as an established fact." Russell heartily agreed. If a mediation attempt failed, "we ought ourselves to recognise the Southern States as an independent State."

The distinct British move toward intervention all but guaranteed a conflict with the Union, particularly since the approach under consideration included the French, who thought recognition the certain outcome of a failed mediation. The implication was clear: both Old World nations considered Confederate independence a foregone conclusion. And regardless of Anglo-French claims to altruistic intentions, the truth was that mediation rested on the premise of a divided United States and that recognition formally designated the South as a nation. The Union, with justification, would regard either action as hostile interference in American domestic affairs and accuse the interventionists of allying with the South. Whether or not a formal partnership, the mere act of intervention could in no way help the North, just as it could in no way hurt the South. Indeed, recognition would open southern commercial and military avenues with other nations and doubtless assure the Union's dissolution. The Lincoln administration would have no recourse other than a humiliating acceptance of European intervention or a war against England that might involve other nations on the European continent and hence prove disastrous to the Union.

But before the Palmerston ministry could initiate the procedure leading to a mediation offer, news reached London of Lee's daring raid into Maryland. Whitehall's diplomatic machinery came to an abrupt halt as government leaders took stock of the new situation and pondered the wisdom of waiting for additional Confederate victories that might, at long last, convince the Union of the impossibility of subjugating the South.

Victory at Fredericksburg Brings the South Close to Independence

J.G. Randall and David Donald

In their book *The Civil War and Reconstruction*, J.G. Randall and David Donald, two prominent Civil War–era historians, discuss a point in late 1862 when the South was confident of victory in the war. In December 1862, at the Battle of Fredericksburg, Confederate forces thwarted an invasion of Virginia by Union forces under the command of General Ambrose Burnside. General Burnside ordered a series of frontal assaults against entrenched Confederate troops fortifying the hills outside of Fredericksburg, Virginia, and the result was a terrible Union defeat with disastrously high casualties. The convincing Confederate victory caused euphoria in the South and depression in the North, as Union currency dropped in value and criticism of President Abraham Lincoln's handling of the war became widespread. The South hoped that the great victory at Fredericksburg might result in pressure on the North to end the war and recognize Southern independence.

Less than six weeks after [General Ambrose] Burnside's accession to command he committed one of the colossal blunders of the war in bringing on the disastrous Union defeat at Fredericksburg. Missing his chance to strike [General "Stonewall"] Jackson and [General James] Longstreet ([General Robert E.] Lee's corps commanders) separately with advantage of position, he struck the united Confederate forces at Fredericksburg, where so great was the disadvantage of position that his preponderance of numbers was neutralized.

J.G. Randall and David Donald, *The Civil War and Reconstruction*. Boston: D.C. Heath, 1961.

The Confederates had established part of their force in an almost impregnable position on Marye's Heights west of the city, while the brigade of General T.R.R. Cobb, together with some of Kershaw's men and J.R. Cooke's North Carolinians, maintained an "unapproachable defense" behind a stone wall in the "sunken road" at the base of the hill. The main battle resolved itself into a series of forlorn, desperate Union charges against the withering musketry and artillery fire of the Confederates. Hopeless as was their plight, the Federals charged on with magnificent determination until at nightfall they retired, leaving the field strewn with their dead, which in many cases were piled three deep.

A Disastrous Union Defeat

But these bloody Union assaults in front of Marye's Heights (the Confederate left) were only a part of the battle, for on the Confederate right there were heavy Union attacks against Jackson and desperate efforts were made to turn that side of Lee's line. "Quickly," writes Freeman, "the Confederate batteries opened in reply. Gaps were cut in the charging columns. Windrows of dead were left behind. In a long volley the Confederate infantry opened, claiming grievous toll in every regiment." Burnside's force at Fredericksburg had numbered nearly 114,000 to Lee's 72,000; but the Confederates were so placed that they could have succeeded had they been outnumbered two to one. Burnside lost 12,600 men, of whom 1284 were killed and 9600 wounded; Lee's killed numbered about six hundred and his total loss about 5300.

Depression in the North

With the failure at Fredericksburg the nadir of Northern depression seemed to have been reached. Sorrow caused by the death or mutilation of thousands of brave men turned into rage as the people wondered how so fine a fighting instrument as the Army of the Potomac had been used with such stupid futility. The slump in public credit was evident in the rise of gold to 134, involving the greatest depreciation of the greenback up to that date. Many urged that the South was ready for a reasonable peace and that it was only the obstinacy of the Lincoln administration which prolonged the war; others demanded a yet "more vigorous" policy, for which Lincoln was considered incompetent. Under bitter criticism for his emancipation proclamation and his suspension of the habeas corpus privilege, Lincoln was under attack from the moderates; and now the Radicals turned upon him and precipitated the most serious cabinet crisis of his ad-

The Wounded from Fredericksburg

Louisa May Alcott, the author of Little Women *and other novels, served as a Union hospital nurse in Washington, D.C., during the Civil War. In her memoir* Hospital Sketches, *Alcott describes Union soldiers brought to her hospital after being wounded in the Battle of Fredericksburg, a devastating defeat for the Union army under the command of General Ambrose Burnside.*

The sight of several stretchers, each with its legless, armless, or desperately wounded occupant, entering my ward, admonished me that I was there to work, not to wonder or weep; so I corked up my feelings, and returned to the path of duty, which was rather "a hard road to travel" just then. The house had been a hotel before hospitals were needed, and many of the doors still bore their old names; some not so inappropriate as might be imagined, for that ward was in truth a *ball-room*, if gun-shot wounds could christen it. Forty beds were prepared, many already tenanted by tired men who fell down anywhere, and drowsed till the smell of food roused them. Round the great stove was gathered the dreariest group I ever saw—ragged, gaunt and pale, mud to the knees, with bloody bandages untouched since put on days before; many bundled up in blankets, coats being lost or useless; and all wearing that disheartened look which proclaimed defeat, more plainly than any telegram of the [General Ambrose] Burnside blunder. I pitied them so much, I dared not speak to them, though, remembering all they had been through since the fight at Fredericksburg.

Louisa May Alcott, *Hospital Sketches.* Chester, CT: Applewood Books, 1990.

ministration. With the army so distrustful of its commander that it seemed on the verge of disintegration, the luckless Burnside asked Lincoln to dismiss or degrade some of the best officers, including Brooks, Hooker, Newton, Cochrane, and Franklin. Their only offense was lack of faith in Burnside himself, a sentiment which pervaded the whole army. Burnside was now considering another thrust across the Rappahannock; but his chances were so doubtful that the President restrained him. Meanwhile Halleck's assistance in reaching a decision as to Burnside's proposed move had proved disappointing. The President wrote: "If in such a difficulty . . . you do not help, you fail me precisely in the point for which I sought your assistance. . . . Your military skill is useless to me if you will not do this." Halleck tendered his resignation, which was not accepted; and Burnside's crossing of the Rappahannock was approved. It resulted in nothing except a wretched "mud march" which began on January 21, the army floundering in floods of rain and seas of sticky clay without making any progress in its purpose of attacking Lee. Another change was imperative. On January 25, 1863, Lincoln removed Burnside and put General Joseph Hooker in command of the Army of the Potomac.

The spring of 1863 came; and as the people looked back upon two years of bungling and sanguinary warfare neither of the struggling sections could point to gains comparable to the losses incurred. The conflict had reached proportions never dreamed of in 1861; fate had supplied a ghastly sequel to the confident predictions and generalizations in which the politicians of that far-off year had indulged. Adjustments that seemed easy in 1861 were out of the question now; neither side could see its way clear to a termination of the struggle. As to generals the advantage was clearly with the Confederacy. At a time when Southern enthusiasm for Lee and Jackson was unbounded, Lincoln wrote his new army chieftain a curious, fatherly letter in which he confessed that he was "not quite satisfied" with him, counseled him to "Beware of rashness," and wistfully besought him to "go forward, and give us victories."

Chapter 3

The North Gains the Advantage

Turning | Points
IN WORLD HISTORY

Turning Points in the War: The Battle of Antietam and Emancipation

James M. McPherson

In September 1862, Confederate General Robert E. Lee led his Army of Northern Virginia on a campaign into Northern territory. At Antietam Creek near Sharpsburg, Maryland, Lee's troops encountered the Army of the Potomac, led by Union General George B. McClellan. On September 17, the two armies fought the bloodiest one-day battle of the Civil War. Combined casualties numbered more than twenty-three thousand men. After the battle, Lee retreated back to Virginia. Having stopped Lee's invasion, the North declared the Battle of Antietam a great victory for the Union. Five days after the battle, President Abraham Lincoln issued the Preliminary Emancipation Proclamation, which notified the South that he would free all slaves in the rebellious states on January 1, 1863. According to James M. McPherson, the author of *Battle Cry of Freedom: the Civil War Era, Abraham Lincoln and the Second American Revolution*, and other seminal texts on the Civil War, the Battle of Antietam turned the tide of the Civil War in the North's favor. The Union victory stopped Lee's invasion, dissuaded European powers from recognizing the Confederacy, and prompted Lincoln to emancipate the slaves. McPherson discusses the effects of the Battle of Antietam in this excerpt from his book *Crossroads of Freedom: Antietam*.

On September 13 [1862] President Lincoln had taken an hour out of his crisis schedule to meet with a delegation of

Chicago clergymen bearing a petition urging a proclamation of emancipation. Lincoln did not tell them that a draft of such a proclamation had rested in a desk drawer for almost two months while he waited for the military situation to improve. That situation had instead gotten worse—and never more so than at that moment when [General Robert E.] Lee was in Maryland, [General George] McClellan had not confronted him yet, panic reigned in much of the North, and the war seemed on the verge of being lost. Lincoln's private secretary John Hay recalled this period as one of "fearful anxiety" and "almost unendurable tension" for the president.

Some of that tension spilled over into his remarks to the delegation, which had claimed that emancipation was the will of God. "If it is probable that God would reveal his will to others, on a point so connected with my duty," said Lincoln testily, "it might be supposed he would reveal it directly to me." In present circumstances, with Rebel armies in Maryland and Kentucky and threatening Pennsylvania and Ohio, "what *good* would a proclamation of emancipation from me do . . . when I cannot even enforce the Constitution in the rebel States? . . . I don't want to issue a document the whole world will see must necessarily be inoperative, like the Pope's bull against the comet!"

A week later all had changed. Five days after [the Battle of] Antietam Lincoln called a special meeting of the Cabinet. He reminded members of their decision two months earlier to postpone issuance of an emancipation proclamation. "I think the time has come now," the president continued. "I wish it was a better time. . . . The action of the army against the rebels has not been quite what I should have best liked. But they have been driven out of Maryland." When the enemy was at Frederick, Lincoln had made a "promise to myself and (hesitating a little) to my Maker" that "if God gave us the victory in the approaching battle, [I] would consider it an indication of Divine will" in favor of emancipation. Perhaps recalling his conversation with the Chicago clergymen, Lincoln suggested that Antietam was God's sign that "he had decided this question in favor of the slaves." Therefore, said the president, he intended that day to issue the proclamation warning Confederate states that unless they returned to the Union by January 1, 1863, their slaves "shall be then, thenceforward, and forever free."

A Change in the Purpose of the War

Perhaps no consequence of Antietam was more momentous than this one. It changed the character of the war, as General-in-Chief [Henry] Halleck noted in a communication to Ulysses S. Grant: "There is now no possible hope of reconciliation. . . . We must conquer the rebels or be conquered by them. . . . Every slave withdrawn from the enemy is the equivalent of a white man put *hors de combat*." The proclamation would apply only to states in rebellion, which produced some confusion because it thus seemed to "liberate" those slaves who were mostly beyond Union authority while leaving in bondage those in the border states. This apparent anomaly caused disappointment among some abolitionists and radical Republicans. But most of them recognized that the commander in chief's legal powers extended only to *enemy* property. Some of that "property," however, *would* be freed by the Proclamation or by the practical forces of war because thousands of contrabands in Confederate states were already within Union lines.

And in any event, the symbolic power of the Proclamation changed the war from one to restore the Union into one to destroy the old Union and build a new one purged of human bondage. "GOD BLESS ABRAHAM LINCOLN!" blazoned Horace Greeley's *New York Tribune* on September 23. "It is the beginning of the end of the rebellion; the beginning of the new life of the nation." The Emancipation Proclamation "is one of those stupendous facts in human history which marks not only an era in the progress of the nation, but an epoch in the history of the world." Speaking for African Americans, Frederick Douglass declared: "We shout for joy that we live to record this righteous decree."

Opposition to Emancipation

Democrats almost unanimously denounced the Proclamation and vowed to campaign against it in the fall congressional elections. Many border-state Unionists also complained loudly. Lincoln had already discounted this opposition, which had once concerned him so greatly. He had tried in vain to get the border states to move voluntarily, but now "we must make the forward movement" without them, he told the Cabinet. "They [will] acquiesce, if not immediately, soon." As for the Democrats, "their clubs would be used against us take what course we might."

Robert E. Lee Realizes the Meaning of His Defeat at Antietam

On September 17, 1862, in the bloody Battle of Antietam, fought near Sharpsburg, Maryland, Union troops repulsed an invasion of Maryland launched by General Robert E. Lee. In his book on this decisive battle, Landscape Turned Red: The Battle of Antietam, *Civil War historian Stephen W. Sears describes Lee as he absorbs the meaning of his defeat.*

Finally, it became clear even to Lee that the Army of Northern Virginia had been fearfully wounded in spirit as well as in body at Sharpsburg. Since early August he had driven his men ruthlessly toward that elusive goal of a decisive victory that might spell Southern independence. Now they could be driven no more. "The whole of our time is taken up by two things, marching and fighting," Brigadier Dorsey Pender of [Confederate General] A.P. Hill's division wrote his wife on September 22. "Some of the army have a fight nearly every day, and the more we fight, the less we like it." The one opinion he had heard about the Maryland invasion, he continued, was "regret at our having gone there." On September 25, outlining his thoughts for a renewed offensive to Mr. [Jefferson] Davis, Lee wrote, "I would not hesitate to make it even with our diminished numbers, did the army exhibit its former temper and condition; but, as far as I am able to judge, the hazard would be great and a reverse disastrous. I am, therefore, led to pause."

Stephen W. Sears, *Landscape Turned Red: The Battle of Antietam*. New York: Warner Books, 1983, p. 340.

More serious, perhaps, was the potential for opposition in the army, especially by McClellanite officers in the Army of the Potomac. There was good reason for worry about this. General Fitz-John Porter branded Lincoln's document "the absurd proclamation of a political coward." It has "caused disgust, and expressions of disloyalty, to the views of the administration" in the army, wrote Porter privately. McClellan himself considered the Proclamation "infamous" and told his wife that he could not "make up my mind to fight for such an accursed doctrine as that of a servile insurrection." McClellan consulted Democratic friends in New York, who advised him "to submit to the Presdt's proclamation & quietly continue doing my duty as a soldier." He even took action to quiet loose talk among some of his subordinates about marching on Washington to overthrow the government. On October 7 McClellan issued a general order reminding the army of its duty of obedience to civil authority. "The remedy for political errors, if any are committed," he noted in a none-too-subtle reference to the forthcoming elections, "is to be found in the action of the people at the polls."

The issue of emancipation would continue—at times dangerously—to divide the army and the Northern public for another six months or more. But in the end, as the *Springfield* (Mass.) *Republican* predicted on September 24, 1862, it would "be sustained by the great mass of the loyal people." These were the people who agreed with Lincoln's words in his message to Congress on December 1, 1862: "Without slavery the rebellion could never have existed; without slavery it could not continue." The *Springfield Republican* proved to be right when it anticipated that "by the courage and prudence of the President, the greatest social and political revolution of the age will be triumphantly carried through in the midst of a civil war."

An Impact Abroad

The battle of Antietam and the Emancipation Proclamation had a signal impact abroad. Only two days before the first news of Antietam arrived in London, the Earl of Shaftesbury,

Prime Minister Palmerston's son-in-law, told Confederate envoys John Slidell and James Mason that "the event you so strongly desire," a British-French offer of mediation and diplomatic recognition, "is very close at hand." But the news of Union victories in Maryland came as "a bitter draught and a stunning blow" to friends of the Confederacy in Britain, wrote the secretary of the American legation. "They express as much chagrin as if they themselves had been defeated."

The London *Times* certainly was stunned by the "exceedingly remarkable" outcome of Antietam. "An army demoralized by a succession of failures," in the words of a *Times* editorial, "has suddenly proved at least equal, and we may probably say superior, to an army elated with triumph and bent upon a continuation of its conquests." Calling Lee's invasion of Maryland "a failure," the normally pro-Southern *Times* admitted that "the Confederates have suffered their first important check exactly at the period when they might have been thought most assured of victory." Other British newspapers expressed similar sentiments. South Mountain and Antietam restored "our drooping credit here," reported American Minister Charles Francis Adams. Most Englishmen had expected the Confederates to capture Washington, and "the surprise" at their retreat "has been quite in proportion. . . . As a consequence, less and less appears to be thought of mediation and intervention."

Adams's prognosis was correct. Prime Minister Palmerston now backed away from the idea of intervention. The only favorable condition for mediation "would be the great success of the South against the North," he pointed out to Foreign Secretary Russell on October 2. "That state of things seemed ten days ago to be approaching," but with Antietam "its advance has been lately checked." Thus "the whole matter is full of difficulty," and nothing could be done until the situation became more clear. By October 22 it *was* clear to Palmerston that Confederate defeats had ended any chance for successful mediation. "I am therefore inclined to change the opinion I wrote you when the Confederates seemed to be carrying all before them, and I am [convinced] . . . that we must continue merely to be lookers-on till the war shall have taken a more decided turn."

Russell and Gladstone, plus Napoleon of France, did not give up easily. The French asked Britain to join in a proposal for a six-months' armistice in the American war during which the blockade would be lifted, cotton exports would be renewed, and peace negotiations would begin. France also approached Russia, which refused to take part in such an obviously pro-Confederate scheme. On November 12 the British Cabinet also rejected it after two days of discussions in which Secretary for War Sir George Cornewall Lewis led the opposition to intervention. In a letter six days later to King Leopold of Belgium, who favored the Confederacy and supported intervention, Palmerston explained the reasons for Britain's refusal to act. "Some months ago" when "the Confederates were gaining ground to the North of Washington, and events seemed to be in their favor," an "opportunity for making some communication" appeared imminent. But "the tide of war changed its

The Battle of Antietam was the bloodiest one-day battle of the Civil War. Pictured above are Confederate soldiers awaiting burial after the battle.

course and the opportunity did not arrive."

Most disappointed of all by this outcome was James Mason, who was left cooling his heels by the British refusal to recognize his own diplomatic status as well as that of his government. On the eve of the arrival in London of news about Antietam, Mason had been "much cheered and elated" by initial reports of Lee's invasion. "Recognition is not far off," he had written on October 1st. Dashed hopes soured Mason on the "obdurate" British, and he felt "that I should terminate the mission here." He decided to stay on, but never again did his mission come so close to success as in September 1862. . . .

Even though the final Proclamation exempted states or parts of states containing one-quarter of all slaves, it nevertheless announced a new war aim that foreshadowed universal emancipation if the North won the war. A black Methodist clergyman in Washington, Henry M. Turner, rejoiced that "the time has come in the history of this nation, when the downtrodden and abject black man can assert his rights, and feel his manhood. . . . The first day of January, 1863, is destined to form one of the most memorable epochs in the history of the world."

As recognition of this truth dawned across the Atlantic, huge mass meetings in Britain adopted pro-Union resolutions and sent copies to the American legation—some fifty of them in all. "The Emancipation Proclamation has done more for us here than all our former victories and all our diplomacy," wrote Henry Adams from London on January 23. "It is creating an almost convulsive reaction in our favor all over this country." The largest of the meetings, at Exeter Hall in London, "has had a powerful effect on our newspapers and politicians," wrote Richard Cobden, one of the foremost pro-Union members of Parliament. "It has closed the mouths of those who have been advocating the side of the South. Recognition of the South, by England, whilst it bases itself on Negro slavery, is an impossibility." Similar reports came from elsewhere in Europe. "The anti-slavery position of the government is at length giving us a substantial foothold in European circles," wrote the American minister

to the Netherlands. "Everyone can understand the significance of a war where emancipation is written on one banner
and slavery on the other.". . .

A Battle with Momentous Consequences

The victory at Antietam could have been more decisive. The
same was true of two lesser victories that followed at Corinth
and Perryville. But Union armies had stymied the supreme
Confederate efforts. Foreign powers backed away from intervention and recognition, and never again came so close to
considering them. Lincoln issued his Emancipation Proclamation. Northern voters chastised but did not overthrow the
Republican party, which forged ahead with its program to
preserve the Union and give it a new birth of freedom. Here
indeed was a pivotal moment.

No other campaign and battle in the war had such momentous, multiple consequences as Antietam. In July 1863
the dual Union triumphs at Gettysburg and Vicksburg
struck another blow that blunted a renewed Confederate offensive in the East and cut off the western third of the Confederacy from the rest. In September 1864 Sherman's capture of Atlanta reversed another decline in Northern morale
and set the stage for the final drive to Union victory. These
also were pivotal moments. But they would never have happened if the triple Confederate offensives in Mississippi,
Kentucky, and most of all Maryland had not been defeated
in the fall of 1862.

Contemporaries recognized Antietam as the preeminent
turning point of the war. Jefferson Davis was depressed by
the outcome there because the Confederacy had put forth its
maximum effort and failed. Two of the war's best corps
commanders, who fought each other at Antietam (and several other battlefields), Winfield Scott Hancock for the
Union and James Longstreet for the Confederacy, made the
same point. In 1865 Hancock looked back on the past four
years and concluded that "the battle of Antietam was the
heaviest disappointment the rebels had met with. They then
felt certain of success and felt that they should carry the war
so far into the Northern states that the recognition of the

Confederacy would have been a necessity." And twenty years after the war, Longstreet wrote simply: "At Sharpsburg was sprung the keystone of the arch upon which the Confederate cause rested." Only with the collapse of that arch could the future of the United States as one nation, indivisible and free, be assured.

Freeing the Slaves and Enrolling Them in the Union Army Spurred the North to Victory

William L. Barney

William L. Barney, a professor of history at the University of North Carolina, is the author of *Battleground for the Union: The Era of the Civil War and Reconstruction, 1848–1877* and *Flawed Victory: A New Perspective on the Civil War*. In this excerpt from *Battleground for the Union*, Barney argues that President Abraham Lincoln's decision to free the slaves on January 1, 1863, and allow African Americans to enroll in the Union army broke a stalemate in the Civil War. Freeing the slaves redefined the purpose of the war—from a conflict to reunite the severed Union to a crusade to rid the United States of slavery forever. After Lincoln signed the Emancipation Proclamation, European nations decided not to recognize or aid the Confederacy. Lincoln's invitation to African Americans to join the Union army resulted in the enlistment of more than 180,000 additional Union troops, a fresh supply of manpower for the North at a critical time in the conflict. Although many Northerners doubted that African Americans would make good soldiers, the new troops performed well on the battlefield, justifying Lincoln's decision to recruit them for the Union war effort.

The Emancipation Proclamation of January 1, 1863, and its accompanying call for the arming of ex-slaves were the major strategic steps taken by [Abraham] Lincoln to break the military stalemate of the first half of the war. Cited by Jefferson Davis as additional proof that the Union was now

William L. Barney, *Battleground for the Union: The Era of the Civil War and Reconstruction, 1848–1877*. Englewood Cliffs, NJ: Prentice-Hall, 1990. Copyright © 1990 by Prentice-Hall, Inc. All rights reserved. Reproduced by permission of the author.

waging the war for "no other purpose than revenge and thirst for blood and plunder of private property," the Emancipation Proclamation did in fact mark the point at which the Union focused the war against the property of planters. It also gave the Union cause a moral purpose in a war effort that earlier could be criticized as a naked grab for power. Friends of the Union in Europe received a tremendous emotional boost, and any chance of European recognition of the Confederacy was greatly reduced. And arming the freed slaves, as Lincoln predicted in March 1863, enabled the North to utilize "the great *available* and yet *unavailed* of, force for restoring the Union."

Interpreted in the South as a declaration of total war, the Emancipation Proclamation had the effect of redoubling Confederate efforts to achieve by force of arms a total and irrevocable separation from the Union. In the spring of 1863, the Confederate Congress belatedly passed its first comprehensive program of taxation to finance the war, Union offensives in the West remained stalled, and Lee's Army of Northern Virginia appeared more invincible than ever after its victory at Chancellorsville, Virginia, in May. Yet . . . the pieces of the Union's victorious war plans had fallen into place by 1863. By simultaneously freeing and arming the slaves, the Union had gained the moral and military momentum in the war. Its strategy of holding in the East, winning in the West, and grinding away everywhere at the Southern social fabric left the Confederacy with neither the space, the material, nor the men it needed to maintain its independence. By the spring of 1865 the Union had bludgeoned the Confederacy into submission.

More Manpower for the Union

"It may have been indecisive, but our resources will stand the wear and tear of indecisive conflict longer than those of slavedom, and can sooner be repaired. . . ." This comment by the New Yorker George Templeton Strong concerning the battle of Murfreesboro (or Stone's River), fought on the last day of 1862 and the second day of 1863, was a shrewd assessment of the standoff in the first two years of the war and its future implications. The biggest battle in the West since Shiloh had just been fought, and the result was another bloody draw that further drained a diminishing Confederate resource base.

General William Rosecrans, the Union commander of the Army of the Cumberland, had replaced Buell after Perryville and was under orders to drive Bragg's Confederate army out of central Tennessee before the winter rains put an end to offensive campaigning. Determined to fight and gain a victory to salvage his Kentucky campaign, Bragg made his stand near Murfreesboro, Tennessee. After initially collapsing the federal right wing, Bragg's attack bogged down on the federal left. The armies rested for a day, and on January 2 Bragg ordered a senseless charge on a Union position east of Stone's River that was covered by the massed fire of the Union artillery. It was a ferocious battle. The sounds of the cannons could be heard twenty-six miles away, and Union soldiers later counted 150 bullets embedded in a two-foot diameter oak that was on the battle site. Yet, Bragg had gained nothing. He had lost one-third of his army killed and wounded, was out of supplies, and had to retreat southward to winter quarters in Tullahoma, Tennessee. Meanwhile, Rosecrans was quickly reinforced, and Middle Tennessee remained open to the federals.

Both before and after Murfreesboro, Rosecrans's army was plagued by Confederate raiders and guerrillas striking at its supply lines. This was a common problem of all Union generals, and it necessitated a huge deployment of troops that was out of all proportion to the amount of enemy territory actually secured by Union offensives. For example, to protect the federal enclave in northern Mississippi and west Tennessee early in 1863, 51,000 Union troops were needed to guard railroads and other lines of communication from a potential Confederate force of about 13,000. Similarly, 43,000 Confederates were able to pin down close to 200,000 federals in Missouri and Arkansas. Even at the end of 1862, at a time when the Union had regained from the Confederacy only the Carolina coast, west Tennessee, northern Arkansas, and the lower Mississippi Valley in the immediate vicinity of New Orleans, these demands for what was essentially garrison duty were already enormous. They could only intensify as Union armies pushed deeper into the South.

As Lincoln wrestled with the problem of emancipation in the last half of 1862, he also worried over how he could ever meet the spiraling demands on Union manpower for both combat and logistical duties. By linking emancipation with arming the ex-slaves, he hit upon one possible solution. The Emancipation Proclamation stipulated that, henceforth, freed slaves would be accepted by the Union military "to garrison forts, positions, stations, and other places, and to man vessels of all sorts in said service."

The Emancipation Proclamation Redefines the War

As a moral document, the Emancipation Proclamation fell far short of a ringing declaration on behalf of human freedom. Critics immediately pointed out that the Proclamation freed slaves in areas where the Union had no authority and kept them enslaved in areas that were under effective Union control. Consistent with Lincoln's belief that emancipation was constitutional only under the war powers of the executive, the Proclamation declared free only those slaves in the Confederacy. Excluded from its provisions were slaves in the loyal states of the Border South and those in the Union-occupied areas of Tennessee, West Virginia, New Orleans and its surrounding parishes, and Norfolk and Virginia's eastern shore.

The Emancipation Proclamation did not free a single slave on the day it was issued, but that was never Lincoln's intention. The purpose of the Proclamation was to redefine the Union's war aims in such a way as to add to Union strength while subtracting from that of the Confederacy. Never forgetting that Union strength had to be defined in political as well as military terms, Lincoln deliberately cast his revolutionary decree in dry, legalistic language that substituted cool military logic for the warmth of moral ardor. Despite this language, Lincoln did disarm his critics on the left by publicly identifying the cause of the Union with the principles of the Declaration of Independence; and because of that language, he assured his critics on the right that he was no wild-eyed radical, but a cautious military strategist who would augment the strength of the military while dismantling slavery.

There was no need to include the loyal slave states of the Upper South in the Proclamation because, as Lincoln repeatedly had told the planters there, the very wear and tear of the war was irreversibly destroying slavery outside the limits of the Confederacy. The Proclamation speeded up this process of disintegration by authorizing the enlistment of black troops. Within a year, efforts in the Border states to limit this recruitment first to free blacks and then to slaves of rebel owners collapsed as a result of the military's insatiable demand for manpower and the desire of nonslaveholding whites to fill their states' draft quotas with as many blacks as possible. In October 1863, the War Department officially sanctioned recruitment practices that had been going on for months. Now, the military could legally recruit all blacks in the Border states, and compensation was to be paid to loyal owners where slaves had enlisted without their permission. Late in the war, Maryland and Missouri provided for emancipation in their state constitutions. Kentucky

This drawing depicts African Americans rejoicing at the Emancipation Proclamation, held by President Abraham Lincoln at left.

and Delaware refused to face reality, and legal, as opposed to *de facto*, emancipation here had to await the passage of the 13th Amendment in 1865.

Europe Reacts to Emancipation

In its most immediate impact, the Emancipation Proclamation all but clinched the case against foreign recognition of the Confederacy. Reaction in Europe to the Civil War loosely followed class lines. European aristocrats, for whom democracy was synonymous with mob rule and an end of legal privilege, generally sympathized with the Confederate cause as the noble effort of a conservative landed elite to break free from the radical excesses of American democracy. Workers, on the other hand, identified with the Union as the embodiment of those principles of liberty and equality that were at the heart of European liberalism and the workers' movement for greater political democracy. These workers embraced the Emancipation Proclamation as an affirmation of the Union's commitment to the rights and dignity of free labor throughout the world. They organized mass protest meetings demanding that their governments remain neutral in a war that could now be characterized as a great moral struggle against the evils of human bondage. Henry Adams, the son of Charles Francis Adams, the American minister to England, reported from London that the Proclamation was a "God-send" in rallying support for the Union.

> I never quite appreciated the "moral influence" of American democracy, nor the cause that the privileged classes in Europe have to fear us, until I saw directly how it works. At this moment, the American question is organising a vast mass of the lower orders in direct contact with the wealthy. They go our whole platform and are full of the "rights of man."

Such talk of universal rights frightened European aristocrats the same way talk of emancipation terrified American slaveholders. To protect their privileged status at home, they pulled back from their espousal of the Confederacy. Led by Britain, Europe would remain on the sidelines barring a major Confederate breakthrough.

The Recruitment of Black Troops

In longer terms, the Emancipation Proclamation was of critical importance in the meeting of Lincoln's manpower goals for the Union military. Although the first black troops were mustered into service in the fall of 1862, recruitment did not begin in earnest until the spring of 1863. Enlistment drives were organized in the Mississippi Valley and the sea-islands, the federally occupied areas with the largest concentration of slaves. Many Union recruiters virtually dragooned able-bodied black males into the army, but, generally, blacks welcomed the chance to fight for their freedom and for that of their families. As Solomon Bradley of South Carolina put it: "In Secesh times I used to pray the Lord for this opportunity to be released from bondage and to fight for my liberty, and I could not feel right so long as I was not in the regiment."

In the North, free blacks enlisted at a rate three times higher than that of whites. Within the South the highest rates of black military participation (close to sixty percent of those eligible) occurred in the loyal Border states. Enrollment in the army brought the freedom that had not been included in the Emancipation Proclamation, and in March 1865 Congress conferred freedom on the families of the black soldiers. Eventually, 180,000 blacks served in the Union army, and four-fifths of them had been slaves at the start of the war.

The arming of the blacks was the logical culmination of a federal policy designed to resolve the problem of what to do with the massive numbers of fugitive slaves who sought the protection of Union armies and navies. By the war's end, half a million slaves had made it behind Union lines. Federal military authorities herded them into makeshift contraband camps. The lack of any federal tradition of responsibility for individual social and economic welfare, the resentment of Union commanders over being burdened with the care of a large class of noncombatants, and the brutal callousness of Union soldiers toward a race they deemed as inferior all contributed to the appalling conditions in these refugee centers. Crowded together in unsanitary conditions where epidemics took a heavy toll, the contrabands suffered mortality rates in excess of twenty-five percent.

Through a process of trial and error, a federal contraband policy took shape in 1862 and 1863. It aimed both at restoring the maximum military efficiency of Union armies and demonstrating to Northern voters that the unraveling of slavery would contribute to a Union victory. The core of this policy was the decision to put the black refugees to work. Battalions of blacks were organized for the heavy, physical work of chopping wood, hauling supplies, and building fortifications. Their wages, which were often late in being paid, were one-third to one-fifth of what black laborers could earn in civilian employment.

Freed Slaves: A Rural Workforce

A far greater number of contrabands were put to work growing cotton. Virtually driven back to the plantations by army commanders, these blacks worked for loyal Southern planters, Northerners who leased abandoned plantations from the federal government, or for the government itself on land placed under the control of freedmen's aid societies in the North. Working conditions were best on the plantations operated by the Northern benevolent societies and their superintendents, but, in nearly all cases, the wages were so low that the freedmen wound up with little more than room and board in return for their labor. This was a free labor system that at the worst approximated slavery.

Still, in terms of the Union war effort, this policy of reestablishing the blacks as a rural work force in the occupied areas of the South was a success. Federal armies were freer to engage in military operations, the cotton-starved textile mills of New England were partially resupplied, and Northern reformers were able to proclaim that black labor could indeed be profitable without the coercive controls of slavery.

This contraband labor policy had the great political virtue of reassuring a worried Northern public that the freed slaves would be contained within the South. Although most blacks had no desire of moving to the North, the possibility of such a black migration and the competition it would touch off for jobs frightened many Northern whites. Sporadic anti-black riots in Northern cities and throughout the lower Ohio Val-

President Lincoln Defends the Emancipation Proclamation and the Enlistment of African American Troops

On January 1, 1863, President Abraham Lincoln signed the Emancipation Proclamation, which freed the slaves in the rebellious Southern states, and invited African Americans to enlist in the Union army. Eight months later, Lincoln defended his Emancipation Proclamation in a letter to James C. Conkling of Illinois.

I thought that in your struggle for the Union, to whatever extent the Negroes should cease helping the enemy, to that extent it weakened the enemy in his resistance to you. Do you think differently? I thought that whatever the Negroes can be got to do as soldiers, leaves just so much less for white soldiers to do, in saving the Union. Does it appear otherwise to you? But Negroes, like other people, act upon motives. Why should they do any thing for us, if we will do nothing for them? If they stake their lives for us, they must be prompted by the strongest motive—even the promise of freedom. And the promise being made, must be kept.

Abraham Lincoln, *Selected Speeches and Writings.* New York: Vintage Books, 1992, p. 392.

ley in 1862 and 1863 convinced Lincoln that the political needs of his party and the avoidance of a racial explosion demanded a federal policy that would keep the blacks within the South. Ultimately, and as Lincoln so clearly saw by the midpoint of the war, the reservoir of black manpower drawn to federal armies in the South could best serve the Union cause as a source of combat soldiers. The mobilization of young black males into Union armies not only minimized any possibility of a war-induced migration of blacks into the North, it also hastened the day on which white Union soldiers in the South would be able to return to their homes in the North.

Arming the Blacks Resulted in a Union Victory

Defeated Confederates later insisted that the Union had never licked them in a fair fight but instead had to enlist the help of blacks in order to win the war. After allowances are made for the wounded pride of white Southerners, that argument stands as a pretty fair assessment of the impact of arming the blacks. The military contributions of blacks were a vital, if not indispensable, element in Union victory. One in eight federal soldiers at the war's end was a black man, and the number of blacks who fought for the Union was larger than the available manpower in Confederate armies as of January 1, 1865.

These numbers alone, however, tell only part of the story. Reliance on black troops helped sustain Northern morale and depress that of the Confederacy. Lincoln turned to black recruitment when white volunteering was at a standstill and a Union draft was about to be instituted in March 1863.

Under the procedures of the draft, each congressional district was assigned a quota of volunteers, and the draft would be implemented only if that quota were not filled within fifty days of each fresh call for troops. As the war dragged on, Northern localities increasingly filled their quotas with blacks recruited in the South by state agents. This substitution of nonlocal blacks for local whites as combat soldiers lightened the burden of the war in the North and thus boosted morale, which had become dangerously low by the spring of 1863. The reverse side of the coin was the demoralization that spread throughout the Confederacy as Southern whites realized that the North was tapping a huge manpower reserve in their former slaves and arming those slaves against them.

Much to the surprise of most whites, blacks quickly proved their effectiveness as combat soldiers in such battles as Milliken's Bend, Fort Wagner, and Petersburg. Nonetheless, and in line with Lincoln's original thinking on the deployment of black troops, blacks were used primarily for garrison and rear-guard duty. Their main role was to free whites for combat service, and they were often stationed in districts where white troops had been decimated by yellow fever and malaria. Such assignments, as well as the inadequate medical treatment that black troops received, largely accounted for a black mortality rate that was forty percent higher than that of white Union soldiers.

High Risks for Black Soldiers

On top of their greater risk of dying in the war, black troops were also discriminated against in terms of pay and access to officers' commissions. White privates received twice the pay ($13 a month plus $3 allowance for clothing) than black soldiers of any rank ($10 a month minus $3 for clothing) until Congress equalized military salaries in June 1864, retroactive to the start of the year. With very few exceptions, commissions in the segregated black regiments were reserved for whites, a policy designed to raise white morale by providing opportunities for rapid advancement. If captured by Confederates, blacks ran the risk of being executed under Southern laws for inciting slave insurrections. Although this threat was rarely carried out, perhaps because Lincoln promised to retaliate in kind by executing Confederate prisoners of war on a one-to-one basis, blacks attempting to surrender were massacred by Confederates at Fort Pillow, Tennessee, and Plymouth, North Carolina, in 1864.

Blacks paid a heavy price in acting as their own liberators. More than one-third of the black soldiers died during their military service. The gains, however, were commensurately great. Blacks now had a claim on the Union that they could present in their demands for full equality and citizenship at the end of the war. After all, more than any other single factor, black military participation had tipped the scales against the Confederacy. Resorting to black troops was a revolutionary step in the white-supremacist culture of Civil War America. In taking that step on behalf of the manpower needs of the Union military, Lincoln was justifiably worried about a white backlash. Yet, as Lincoln sensed they would, even many of the rabid racists eventually conceded that black lives might as well be sacrificed along with white ones if it meant the preservation of the Union.

The Battle of Vicksburg Destroyed the Confederacy

James R. Arnold

In the spring of 1863, General Ulysses S. Grant began a military campaign that took his army southward through the Mississippi River Valley into Mississippi. Grant's goal was to gain Union control of the Mississippi River. The key to achieving the goal was the capture of Vicksburg, an important shipping center on the shores of the river. Confederate batteries set on bluffs two hundred feet above the river defended Vicksburg and prevented Union ships from traversing the Mississippi. After winning battlefield victories north of Vicksburg, Grant, in mid-May, began a long siege of Vicksburg that culminated in a Confederate surrender of the city on July 4, 1863. According to Civil War historian James R. Arnold, the author of *Grant Wins the War: Decision at Vicksburg*, from which this article is excerpted, the Union victory at Vicksburg sealed the defeat of the Confederacy. It divided the Confederacy in two and gave the North control of the Mississippi River, which interrupted the South's supply trains and destroyed communication between its eastern and western sections.

The day that [President] Lincoln penned his first letter to [General Ulysses S.] Grant, President Davis wrote a letter of an altogether different tone: "We are now in the darkest hour of our political existence." Midsummer 1863 found the tide of war turning against the Confederacy. The men [General Braxton] Bragg sent to relieve Vicksburg had sufficiently weakened his army so as to encourage [General William] Rosecrans to advance. In nine days of exceptional maneuver,

Rosecrans drove Bragg from Tennessee. On the day Vicksburg surrendered, Bragg's army retreated into Chattanooga. [Generals] Lee, Pemberton, Holmes, and Bragg, the commanders of the South's four major field armies, had all been defeated.

But it was Vicksburg and Gettysburg that captured public attention. At the time, most Southerners considered Vicksburg far more significant. In part, it was a matter of perspective. Lee's soldiers emphasized their success during Gettysburg's first two days and their ability to conduct an orderly return to Virginia. Civilians largely shared this view. At worst, Gettysburg had been a drawn battle. In contrast, everyone recognized the disaster on the Mississippi.

Southern Reactions to Vicksburg

Typical was Georgia governor Joseph Brown. Omitting any mention of Gettysburg, on July 17 he urged his people not to despair over "the late serious disasters to our arms" in Mississippi and Tennessee. Edmund Ruffin, the venerable fire-eater who had touched off the first gun aimed at Fort Sumter, likewise labeled the loss of the Mississippi a disaster. Looking at the map, Southerners saw the country cut in half. Looking to the future, many despaired. A Confederate congressman wrote, "The disastrous movement of Lee into Pennsylvania and the fall of Vicksburg, the latter especially, will end in the ruin of the South . . . the failure of the Government to re-enforce Vicksburg . . . has so broken down the hopes of our people that even the little strength yet remaining can only be exerted in despair." South Carolina infantryman Tally Simpson had marched with Lee's army to Gettysburg and back. Upon hearing of Vicksburg's fall, he wrote home to call it a "hard stroke for the Confederacy." Upon further reflection, he elaborated: "The fall of Vicksburg has caused me to lose confidence in something or somebody."

Whereas eastern Confederate soldiers invested hope in Lee, the westerners had no such lodestar. Tennessee major Flavel Barber contrasted the elation of victory one year before with the situation following Vicksburg's fall: "We still have courage and resolution left but we are fighting more because we know our cause to be just than because we are sanguine of success." A Texas sergeant serving in [Confederate general Joseph] Johnston's army expressed much greater despondency: "I have little hope of the future."

Lee remained uncomprehending about what had taken place on the Mississippi. Once his army limped safely home from its slaughter in Pennsylvania, he assessed affairs in the West. He wrote to Davis that the wisest course now was "to select some point on the Mississippi and fortify it strongly." He elaborated that a small garrison with adequate provisions could hold such works against the type of attack Grant had mounted against Vicksburg. Where such a fort could be built given Federal control of both banks of the river, Lee omitted to mention. How such a fort could restore the severed link to the Trans-Mississippi he did not say.

The Union Gains Control of the Mississippi River

Federal control of the Mississippi separated the Confederacy into two sections. Union patrols along the river interdicted almost all communication between East and West. "Thenceforth," wrote Sherman, the Confederates "could not cross it save by stealth." Illustrative of this fact was the experience of a small group of rebel volunteers who escorted an officer who was trying to travel to Louisiana. This officer had the important duty of carrying 1.5 million Confederate dollars in back pay and 30,000 rounds of ammunition to the Third Louisiana regiment, which had been paroled and re-formed after Vicksburg's surrender. In spite of traveling with an experienced blockade runner, the party spent nearly a month in the Mississippi swamps dodging gunboats and Federal patrols before venturing across the river. In Sherman's words, the complete isolation of West from East rendered military affairs on the west bank "unimportant."

Jefferson Davis knew that this war was a test of wills. Harking back to the days of the American Revolution, he found hope in the rebels' ability to persevere in the face of setback and defeat. In August he told Lee that the Southern people seemed to have quickly recovered from their depression over defeat in the West and were again exhibiting "that fortitude . . . needful to secure ultimate success." A Virginia captain spoke for Davis, Lee, and the soldiers of the Army of Northern Virginia when he wrote his wife that "by God's grace we will soon strike the enemy such a blow, that his hopes of subjugation will be as far off as before the fall of Vicksburg."

If that blow were to be struck, it would be performed by hungry soldiers. An extremely rainy Virginia summer of 1863 ruined the wheat crop. The loss of the Mississippi Valley eliminated the accumulation of molasses and sugar which heretofore had been mixed with other foods and used as a substitute. In Dalton, Georgia, the winter camp of the Army of Tennessee in 1863–1864, a veteran of the campaigning around Vicksburg wrote that the food was the worst yet.

The loss of access to the Trans-Mississippi, along with other Confederate setbacks, drove Richmond officials to ever more draconian measures to procure food for the armies. Government agents bought cattle, hogs, and corn at controlled prices far below the market prices. Furthermore, they used a debased currency to make these purchases. Not surprisingly, planters tried to avoid selling to the government by hiding their produce, declaring they merely had enough for their own use, or, where possible, taking it across Federal lines where they could be paid in greenbacks or gold. In turn, the Confederate government resorted to impressment. Not even conscription caused so much discontent and outright resentment. "This practice," observed General Taylor, "alienates the affections of the people, debauches the troops, and ultimately destroys its own capacity to produce results."

The loss of the Trans-Mississippi's "hogs and hominy" forced the Confederacy to substitute food for war munitions aboard its blockade runners. This measure proved inadequate. During the winter of 1864–1865, Lee's army barely endured on a diet of imported meat from Nassau in the Bahamas. The enervating effects of low-quality "Nausea bacon," as the soldiers called it, substantially reduced army mobility. So bad had the situation become that by the beginning of 1865, the *Southern Cultivator* opined that every possible means must be used to encourage food production: "This war cannot be kept up without food."

Lawlessness in the Mississippi Valley

Back in 1862, Grant and Sherman's plan had been to hold the Mississippi River and leave the interior alone except for occasional raids against the railroads. Sherman had believed that "we could make ourselves so busy that our descent would be dreaded the whole length of the river." Following the fall of Vicksburg, this is what transpired, and the Mississippi Valley became a lawless region. Whereas earlier in the war Southern women had shamed the reluctant to join the army, now that the government had proven unable to keep the enemy at bay, public spirit changed. There remained numerous men of conscription age, but they were finding it ever easier to shelter themselves among a sympathetic population and avoid service. The fringe areas of Confederate control were increasingly overrun with stragglers and deserters, while the state troops assigned to round them up were proving unwilling to force their neighbors back into the ranks. Ironically, Confederate cavalry and provost patrols began using dogs that had been trained to chase escaped slaves to hunt down draft dodgers and deserters. A Louisiana soldier home on leave in November 1863 found the locals carrying on a very active, but illicit, cotton trade with Union-occupied Baton Rouge. Women always carried the cotton, since guards would let them pass. The local Confederate cavalry took regular bribes to allow the trade to continue and earned the name "cotton tollers." Open theft by formed Confederate units was so common that it caused the soldier to lament, "Nearly everybody seemed to have lost all sense of right and wrong."

The capture of Vicksburg also had an immediate impact upon the morale of the Army of the Tennessee. It had never known defeat and Vicksburg seemed to crown its achievements. Consequently, the army fell into an understandable complacency. They had labored hard and risked much. Officers sought home leave, and men obtained furloughs and discharges whenever possible. The ranks thinned, with many regiments becoming mere skeletons. The Federal and state governments seemed loath to enforce the politically unpopular draft to replenish their ranks. The war on the Mississippi was at a natural lull, but it threatened to become a strategic drift, like the one that had occurred after the capture of Corinth the previous year.

General Ulysses S. Grant Turned the Tide of the War

T. Harry Williams

For the first two years of the Civil War, President Abraham Lincoln was forced to deal with ineffective generals at the head of the Union army. Generals George B. McClellan, Ambrose Burnside, Joe Hooker, and others often blundered badly on the battlefield and failed to accomplish Lincoln's goal of destroying the Confederate army and capturing the Confederate capital in Richmond, Virginia. One general, however, in the war's western theater, enjoyed battlefield successes and displayed both verve and brilliant strategy in his campaigns: General Ulysses S. Grant, a West Point graduate and Mexican War veteran. When Lincoln's military advisers questioned Grant's abilities and whispered rumors of a drinking problem, Lincoln, who tolerated for two years generals who were intimidated by Confederate General Robert E. Lee's resourceful Army of Northern Virginia, simply replied, "I can't spare this man; he fights." In the spring and summer of 1863, Grant engineered a campaign that resulted in the capture of Vicksburg, Mississippi, an important river port on the Mississippi River. Shortly thereafter, Lincoln appointed Grant as the commander of all Union forces. Grant immediately began planning the military campaigns that would ultimately defeat the Confederacy. According to Civil War–era historian T. Harry Williams, the author of *Lincoln and His Generals* and other books on the Civil War, Grant "struck the blow that won the war."

T. Harry Williams, *McClellan, Sherman and Grant*. Piscataway, NJ: Rutgers University Press, 1962. Copyright © 1962 by Rutgers, the State University. Reproduced by permission of Ivan R. Dee, publisher.

Vicksburg is one of the classic campaigns of the Civil War and, indeed, of military history. It began with a traditional two-pronged advance from a base at Memphis. This movement failed, but instead of returning to Memphis and beginning a new attack, as the rules dictated, [General Ulysses S.] Grant shifted all his forces to the Mississippi. It turned into an apparent stalemate, with the Federals vainly seeking to approach Vicksburg over the marshy terrain north of the city. In the spring Grant unmasked his real plan, which he had matured in the winter months. Moving his army down the west side of the river while the navy ran by the enemy batteries, he crossed below the city and stood on dry ground. He faced two separate Confederate forces, one at Vicksburg and one at Jackson, which if united would outnumber him. Then the general called dull and unimaginative and a mere hammerer executed one of the fastest and boldest moves in the records of war. He struck the force at his rear and dissipated its threat and closed the one to his front in its fortress. In eighteen days he marched 200 miles, won four battles, and inflicted losses of 8,000 men and 88 guns on the foe.

After this brilliant demonstration the campaign settled into a siege. Tenacity took over from audacity and finally triumphed. Vicksburg fell and Grant rose to the apex of his career. Now there was none to carp. All hailed him as great. He became departmental commander of the whole Western theater, and in 1864 supreme commander over every theater.

Lincoln's Admiration

Unknown to Grant, there was one who had marked him as great before Vicksburg and this individual's opinion was of some importance. As early as [the battles for Forts] Henry and Donelson, Abraham Lincoln had noted that this Western general possessed some pleasingly rare qualities. Lincoln saw to it that Grant was promoted and followed closely the general's continued development. The reason for Lincoln's interest soon became evident. To a suggestion in the aftermath of Shiloh that Grant should be removed, the President replied simply: "I can't spare this man; he fights." Lincoln again sustained Grant during the Vicksburg siege. Some parties contended that Grant was wasting lives in a hopeless operation and should be relieved. Shrugging off the complaints, Lincoln said: "I rather like the man. I think I'll try him a little longer." Lincoln liked Grant for several reasons. Not only would Grant fight, but he fought with the men and the tools he had at hand.

Every general in the war exaggerated the size of the enemy forces and tried to augment his own, and Grant was no exception. But he made his requests quietly, and if he was told that reinforcements were not available he made out with what he had. In this respect he was practically unique among Northern generals. Here was no [General William T.] Sherman collapsing at the specter of hosts gathering to destroy him or no [General George] McClellan always calling shrilly for more men and putting the responsibility for defeat on the government if he did not get them. A typical Grant application to Lincoln ran: "The greater number of men we have, the shorter and less sanguinary will be the war. I give this entirely as my views and not in any spirit of dictation— always holding myself in readiness to use the material given me to the best advantage I know how."

Lincoln was impressed by such restraint. He knew too many generals who wrote much and fought little. Once he remarked gratefully: "General Grant is a copious worker and fighter, but a very meager writer or telegrapher." The President expressed his fullest appreciation of Grant's reticence to a friend just before Vicksburg fell. "He doesn't worry and bother me," Lincoln said. "He isn't shrieking for reinforcements all the time. He takes what troops we can safely give him . . . and does the best he can with what he has got." Then Lincoln added: "And if Grant only does this thing right down there . . . why, Grant is my man and I am his the rest of the war."

Grant Assumes Command

Grant had done it right, and in 1864 he was the man, the central figure in the Union command system. He had demonstrated his capacities in every grade from regimental to departmental command, and now he was to face a greater test.

In his position as supreme commander he would have to formulate strategy for the Union armies on many fronts and to oversee the execution of this strategy. And by his own choice he would direct, although not technically command, the field army that confronted the most dangerous Confederate army commanded by the man that most of the generals under him considered the greatest soldier of the war, Robert E. Lee.

In 1864 Grant stood in the full flower of his generalship. What manner of man was Lincoln's man and what kind of general was Lincoln's general? The man was a curious compound of many things. Outwardly solemn and shy, he could flash forth with bits of humor even in official documents. In the election of 1864 Lincoln through a friend requested permission to use a letter from Grant to prove there had been no presidential interference with army matters. Grant readily agreed to the President's quoting anything he had written but added: "I think, however, for him to attempt to answer all the charges the opposition will bring against him will be

General Ulysses S. Grant enjoyed great battlefield success. Pictured above, Grant holds a council of war in May 1864.

like setting a maiden to work to prove her chastity." Sometimes Grant's wit had a bite to it, as when he said a certain officer would "scarcely make a respectable Hospital nurse, if put in petticoats," or when he recommended that a general whom he disliked be stationed "at some convenient point on the northern frontier with the duty of detecting and exposing rebel conspiracies in Canada."

The man was—and in this he was much like Lincoln—a mixture of iron and velvet. He could send thousands of men into battle and to death without flinching. But he could be tremendously affected by the sight of wounded and especially maimed individuals. He could shatter Confederate armies with unrelenting and unending blows. But nobody was more capable of the knightly gesture to the defeated than this seemingly commonplace man. His conduct at Appomattox was not an inspiration of the moment or an isolated incident. He had manifested the same spirit in previous if lesser scenes. . . .

Grant's Strategy for Victory

Grant would have need of all his strength of character in 1864. As supreme commander he framed a plan of grand strategy to attack the Confederacy on several fronts. He elected to accompany and direct the Federal army advancing on the most important front, the one held by [General Robert E.] Lee and his army. His instructions to Sherman and lesser commanders in other theaters were to make enemy armies their objective, and his directions to [General George] Meade, the titular head of the Eastern army, were the same: "Wherever Lee goes, there you will go also."

Grant traveled with Meade's army, in effect commanded it, for a definite purpose. Lee and Lee's army constituted the principal power of the Confederacy. Regardless of what happened in any other theater, the greatest power of the enemy had to be destroyed. Grant was determined to see to the job personally. He struck Lee in the savage and sustained battle of the Wilderness. It was the first meeting of the two greatest generals of the war, its only two who deserved to be ranked among the battle captains of history. Grant intended to force Lee to a showdown battle that would end the war immediately. He failed and recoiled with ghastly losses. The familiar pattern seemed about to repeat itself. A Federal general had attacked Lee and had been repelled, and now he would retire to lick his wounds, giving the Confederates time to regroup, and later, in weeks or months, he might come on again.

This was Grant's moment of crisis, and he met it. A reporter starting for Washington asked if the general had any message for the country. Grant thought a minute and said he had: "Well, if you see the President, tell him for me that, whatever happens, there will be no turning back." Lincoln caught the import of Grant's decision. "How near we have been to this thing before and failed," he exclaimed to his secretary. "I believe if any other general had been at the head of that army it would have been now on this side of the Rapidan."

Grant turned south after the Wilderness. Weeks and months of battle and siege lay ahead of him before he would achieve his objective of destroying Lee's army. But when he advanced instead of retiring, in that very action he had won the campaign. He refused to let Lee exercise a psychological ascendancy over him, as Lee had over every other Northern general, and he, having the initiative, now had an ascendancy over Lee. Many comparisons of the two great rivals have been made, and such evaluations are instructive. Lee was the better tactician and was more brilliant on the battlefield. Grant was the better strategist and had a broader view of the war. But in their dramatic meeting the decision came down to a question of will. It was a clash of two tremendous wills, two powerful characters. Grant triumphed, not because his will was any stronger than Lee's but because it was as strong and because he had the physical force to impose his will on his opponent. The campaign of 1864 is often treated in terms of numbers and supplies, and the result is attributed to purely material factors. All these played their part, but they would have been as nothing without the direction of a man.

A Final Evaluation

There is no difficulty in composing a final evaluation of Ulysses S. Grant. The summation can be as short as one of his own deceivingly simple statements. With him there need be no balancing and qualifying, no ifs and buts. He won battles and campaigns, and he struck the blow that won the war. No general could do what he did because of accident or luck or preponderance of numbers and weapons. He was a success because he was a complete general and a complete character. He was so complete that his countrymen have never been able to believe he was real.

Why the North Won the Civil War

Phillip Shaw Paludan

In his book *"A People's Contest": The Union and the Civil War, 1861–1865*, Phillip Shaw Paludan, a professor of history at the University of Kansas and the author of *The Presidency of Abraham Lincoln*, speculates on why the North won the Civil War. Paludan identifies several factors responsible for the Union's victory: the North's larger population, its vast economic resources, its established constitutional system, and its war leadership. In addition, in Paludan's view, the North's communities did not suffer as badly as communities in the South because the war was mainly fought on Southern soil. All of these factors worked together to give the North the will to continue to fight the war to its conclusion.

The North won the Civil War because in the largest sense it had the economic, institutional, intellectual, and social resources for victory. The economic resources are obvious: more men, more shops and factories, more tools, more railroads, more ships, even more farms, food, and fiber. Furthermore, it had the knowledge to organize those resources and employ them in the war. Prewar industrialization both required and created men who developed the necessary tools of finance, business, and industry. The growing equation of private advancement with the public interest encouraged public officials to rely on these men to mobilize resources. Private industry for its part believed in its obligation to preserve the nation. The North also relied on workers educated by the public school systems and work experience. They made and repaired the guns and the locomotives, harvested the crops with the new machines, supplying civilians and soldiers with what they needed.

The North's Generals

Northern generals knew how to use material advantages. Most West Pointers did not stay in the army in the antebellum period. They went into private business, where their training in engineering and organization could be used profitably. [General George] McClellan especially had learned as a railroad executive how to forge an efficient and powerful organization, whether that was a railroad or an army. Henry Halleck and Montgomery Meigs similarly had learned in peace how to organize modern war. Grant and Sherman and other Union generals absorbed in prewar experience the nature and potentialities of Northern resources. Southern generals, of course, also knew of those things, but lacked sufficient resources to use the knowledge to mobilize for victory. Northern generals had the means and knew most of the ways.

The large and diverse Northern population also provided vital advantages. It supplied over 2 million enlistments and produced an army of nearly 1 million men by mid-1865. The North, which had welcomed immigration while the South had discouraged it, could call on 500,000 foreign-born troops who were ready to fight. Xenophobia still existed. But the North had sufficient tolerance to accept these 5,000 regiments. While most Northerners considered blacks inferior, they were not afraid to put guns in their hands: 45,000 free blacks from the North were added to the army. And 134,000 more stepped from slavery into soldiering, further swelling Union ranks. Northern needs overcame racial and nativist anxieties.

The North also developed self-images that set the stage for victory. The ideal of social mobility allowed its armies to generate new leadership in the midst of war. The Confederate generals who began the war as leaders kept their positions until the end. The architects of Northern victory sat in comparative obscurity in the conflict's early days. But as the war ground on, Grant and Sherman and Thomas and Sheridan emerged to take the reins. They had a commander in chief who knew from his own experience how to watch for and reward men on the make. The fact that war allowed such men to climb, of course, further endorsed the strength of Northern society.

Political Advantages

Politics contributed another sign of vitality and built self-confidence. Lincoln initially called upon the North to defend the right of changing governments by elections, not secession. The electoral process continued throughout the war. Every election showed that self-government worked in the North. The system was strong enough that in the midst of a challenge to their survival as a nation, they could tolerate, indeed had to tolerate, the turmoil of the election process.

That turmoil strengthened the government. Winners pointed to the support of the people and undercut opposition. Losers by participating showed they believed in the process if not the result. The existence of the ballot box option made defiance appear as disloyalty. The vital two-party system kept opposition within bounds by requiring platforms that spoke to the broad middle of the political spectrum, not to the extremes. It also opened careers and patronage to those ambitious men who played by the rules. A strong opposition, in addition, kept the ruling party unified enough to win elections despite interfamily quarrels.

Lincoln played a vital role in strengthening faith in the political system. He spoke of the principles of self-government constantly—keeping the goal before the people. While there were abuses, Lincoln and his government generally exercised restraint in curbing dissent. Most of his critics were free to damn him for his "dictatorship," and he took pains to provide persuasive constitutional justifications for limiting civil liberties. Example as well as rhetoric persuaded Northerners that their system was worth fighting for.

The constitutional system also proved its strength and helped the Northern war effort. While Lincoln provided a constitutional presidency adequate to defend the nation, congressmen rediscovered the Hamiltonian heritage that used power to defend liberty. Jeffersonian/Jacksonian traditions that denied national power lost influence. A national currency, a national banking system, a national tax structure, all emerged during the war, linking ordinary people to their government in tangible ways, proving that national power paid off for those who had, or aspired to, economic influence. The war emergency both justified and obscured consequent economic inequities. These measures allowed the North to mobilize its wealth to save the nation. That wealth paid the armies, bought the supplies, built the transportation systems, and fed homefront faith in the system.

One reason for the North's victory in the Civil War was that Union soldiers, pictured above, were backed by greater economic resources than Confederates.

The War Congress satisfied factions in the private economy that had been ignored by Democrats with their laissez-faire theories. A Homestead Act opened lands to settlement, providing farms for those with little cash and much hope. The Pacific Railroad Bill linked the West Coast with the rest of the nation and in the process fulfilled white dreams of national grandeur and personal prosperity. Higher tariffs in fact benefited the capitalists who needed protection for infant industry and, theoretically, their workers. The war environment made it possible to believe that their interests were the same. Congress also funded a system of higher education that undeniably helped all segments of the society. Here were signs that the people's government might be their instrument, not their enemy.

Organized resources, emerging generals, a vital political and constitutional system, all built Northern strength that protected the Union in the foreign arena. England and France, the only powers that mattered, became less and less interested in challenging the Union blockade or assisting the Confederacy. The Union might provoke a crisis by challenging foreign powers directly, or by intransigence in settling inevitable disputes. But Seward and Lincoln were wise enough to balance the protection of Union prerogatives with a willingness to negotiate. The secretary of state alternated bombast and reasonableness, while Lincoln watched Seward to make sure that bombast did not dominate. Both men knew when to back away from confrontation and thus gain support by retreat. The strength of the North meant that they would not have to back away too far.

Fighting for Ideals

The North also had the advantage of fighting for ideals that the vast majority of the population agreed with. In Dixie internal opposition to the economic power of slavery produced a fault line running along the Appalachians that could unleash disruption at any time. Some in Dixie doubted the morality of slavery itself. Military defeats and/or the war measures of a desperate government could unleash these feelings and erode the will to fight. The Confederacy was potentially further divided by its abiding state sovereignty philosophy. Differences in Dixie not only were questions of policy; they were matters of the very structure of the republic.

There were also divisions in the North. The great divide was over how much the war cost in lives and in changing the society. Democrats argued against expansion of national power over civil liberties, the alliance between government and the economic power, changing the status of blacks. The draft riots showed how passionate such protest might be. But even though they interpreted liberty and equality and the Constitution in different ways, Northerners still were united by general agreements about their system. Even Vallandigham insisted he was for saving the Union, and every antiwar politician stayed in politics and insisted on his respect for the constitutional system. State sovereignty as a motto was heard in the North, but aside from an occasional state judge who lacked jurisdiction beyond his courtroom, no responsible Northern official ever used the doctrine to restrain national government action. The fact that the rebellion was based on that principle effectively weakened its force in the North. Northerners were nationalists, state rights nationalists in the majority of cases, but still believers in the right of the government to find the means to save itself.

All parties generally agreed on the validity of the economic system, too, and the war strengthened that agreement. Democrats denied that Republican direction of the economy was fair to the ordinary people they claimed to represent. They did not doubt that a Democratically guided economy would prosper. Laborers protested the power of capital in order to gain the right to be capitalists themselves. Northerners did not have to explain or rationalize away their free labor system. Both parties claimed to represent it. As the struggle for the Union and for the free labor system intensified, it stifled most of the latent class consciousness that did exist.

Opposition to slavery also was powerful in the North. In an environment already sensitive to loss of control and morality, the Republican party came to life out of anger that slavery reached out to imperil the Union, erode constitutional liberties, and corrode ideals of equality that had defined the nation in the first place. Racist fears combined with other constitutional imperatives, and love of the Union protected slavery. But the war undercut those protections. Sumter damaged arguments that slavery was the price of union. Securing Kentucky disarmed strategic opposition to emancipation. Black soldiers and laborers undercut racist fears. In this environment Republicans interwove abolitionist arguments about the justness and Christian duty of emancipation with arguments from expediency. Lincoln's eloquence kept alive principles he had spoken in the 1850s: the Union rested on the "standard maxim for a free society," the equality of all men.

As the war continued, therefore, saving the Union and ending slavery were integrated as harmonious goals. Those inclined to separate them began to recognize that their purposes were the same. By 1863 abolition was a popular unifying goal, and that unity increased until, by 1865, Democratic congressmen were voting for the Thirteenth Amendment.

Racism did not die. Its purposes could be sustained by constitutional and social ideas that gained power during the conflict. Nevertheless, during the conflict Northerners built the will to continue fighting in large measure out of the growing consensus that liberty and union were "one and inseparable."

The North also gained strength because its fears and anxieties were focused in positive ways. War answered the doubts of many that the system could produce moral citizens. It proved that men would risk their fortunes and their lives for an unselfish purpose. War provided answers to prewar worries that inequality was growing, opportunity for poorer men contracting. The wartime boom illustrated economic vitality. Its inequities could be explained away as imperative sacrifices for the cause. The widely publicized humble origins of wartime leaders argued that the paths of opportunity were open to hardworking, honest men. Lincoln, Sherman, Grant, and their well-supplied and unrelenting armies of farmers, laborers, and mechanics showed what the industrializing nation was capable of.

The South's Role in the North's Victory

The South played an important role in the Northern victory. Southern strategy essentially left the North alone to discover its vitality and strength. Jefferson Davis and his military advisers understood that they lacked the ability to invade the North. Their best strategy was to defend Dixie until Northern will wore out. An occasional foray above the Mason-Dixon line might be employed in the service of this "offensive-defensive" strategy, but fundamentally the Confederacy could not bring the war to Northern farms, communities, and cities.

The deaths of thousands of young men reminded Northerners constantly that they were engaged in an agonizing, bloody business. But because rebel armies stayed in Dixie, Northerners could stir their fires, send their children off to school, go to work in busy shops and factories, plant and harvest their crops, and, as Ellen Wright said, "make believe a little longer," living the normal lives that the supranormal times both demanded and allowed. The thousands of communities that made up the Union were left alone to generate loyalty and nurture the daily affirmed faith that self-government was worth preserving. Northerners recognized the possibility of temporary military defeat, but the South never challenged the Northern belief that it had the strength to win if it only retained the will to win.

None of these factors alone explains the Northern victory. All worked together to create the will to continue the fight and the means to make that will irresistible. The economy that provided the resources to bring Northern victory generated at the same time anxieties that justified, and at times seemed to demand, war. The shared values of the North were preserved by the fact that fighting and destruction never seriously threatened Northerners' day-to-day lives. Unity thus came with success and success with unity.

Chapter 4

A Changed Nation

The United States Becomes One Nation

Jay Winik

In his book *April 1865: The Month That Saved America*, historian Jay Winik asserts that Union and Confederate political and military leaders at the end of the Civil War set aside their differences and collaborated to save the United States; these leaders accomplished President Abraham Lincoln's goal of molding two essentially separate nations—the Union and the Confederacy—into a single nation. In this excerpt from *April 1865*, Winik explains that the determined men who fought the Civil War succeeded in convincing Northerners and Southerners to become good citizens of a newly united and fundamentally changed nation. In doing so, the wartime leaders of the North and South would create "a diverse and democratic country, inspiring quests for freedom around the globe."

By April 1865, even as it became apparent that the Union was in one manner or another going to win the war, the fate of the country still remained very much in doubt. The conclusions of wars are every bit as crucial as how and why they begin and how and why they are fought. History is littered with the wreckage of bad endings. This was complicated, of course, by the fact that at that moment, the South had also changed. [President] Lincoln had always contended that the South had never left the Union: he spoke of the "so-called Confederacy," insisting that the states had not really seceded from the Union because they could not; he even went as far as to maintain that "the whole country is our soil" and the South still remained in the Union. And further, he said that it was not a war between states but an insurrection, in effect, warranting a large police action. But at best, this logic was little more than a legal technicality (and a debatable one at that), at odds with the reality on the ground, if not wishful thinking on the part of Lincoln. Through its darkest days, from first Manassas to Sayler's Creek, from Fort Sumter to Appomattox and Durham Station, the Confederacy had become something that even the United States itself at its founding was truly not: a separate nation, sharing not simply a common language but a common culture, heritage, identity; common heroes; and, perhaps most importantly, a common sense of destiny. In British statesman William Gladstone's memorable words in 1863: "Jefferson Davis and the other leaders of the South have made an army; they are making, it appears, a navy; and they have made what is more than either, they have made a nation." The unanimity of Confederate nationality may be overstated, but the Union's task of reabsorbing an essentially hostile entity, to which it had just laid siege, should not be. Susan Emiline Jeffords Caldwell, of Virginia, neatly summed up this problem in March 1865: "I want peace but I don't want to go back into the Union. I want *Independence* and nothing else.—I could not consent to go back with a people that has been bent on exterminating us." Nor can the challenge of overcoming deep and abiding enmity be overestimated. Lincoln knew this—it was one of his wisest, greatest insights. That is why he refused to gloat, or smugly indulge in celebration, or demonize his foe. Remarkably, and importantly, on this last point, neither did the leaders of the Confederacy, Robert E. Lee most notably among them.

A Nation Formed from the Debris of War

These men of battle knew that war most often engenders hatred. But by their collective actions in ending the war, they, along with Lincoln, helped to constitute a country. In mid-April, as the cataclysmic events rushed together, when Lee surrendered at Appomattox—"as much to Lincoln's goodness as to Grant's armies," he would say—then Johnston at Durham Station, and then Taylor and Forrest and all the rest followed, they were asking something quite remarkable of the people whom they had just led through four years of bloody battle: to become good citizens of a United States that had thwarted their bid for independence and stymied their urge for self-determination. And above all, Lincoln, and men like [Generals] Grant and Sherman, would call on the North to be equally remarkable, appealing to reconciliation, not vengeance, to common ground, not revenge, to mutual citizenship, not differences.

Would it work? Could it work? The United States was like an enormous jigsaw puzzle whose many pieces could be slowly pulled into place, or irrevocably fall apart. For a while, in fact, a very long while, it had been touch and go. The Civil War was not just a war between states, or an insurrection, but by the end, with the entire institution of slavery overthrown, the South laid waste, setting it back generations, it was also a revolution. And revolutions rarely go quietly. Was this revolution, like Saturn, like so many revolutions, destined to eat its own children, which Lincoln himself had warned against early on? In the fateful days of April 1865, this haunting question would turn on a handful of choices and decisions: what if Lee had found an abundance of food at Amelia Court House—and safely made his way south to link up with [General] Joe Johnston? Or if he had decided that honor lay not in surrendering but in fighting on and on for the mother South—with organized guerrilla warfare? Or if Lee had responded to surrender not with dignity and honor, but with rage? Or if Grant and Sherman had neglected Lincoln's admonitions at City Point and responded not with generosity of spirit, but with unbridled anger? Or if there had not been an honorable stacking of the arms and mutual salute to set the tone for the end of the war, but hangings and humiliation? Or if [Vice President] Andrew Johnson had been assassinated after all—and the blade hadn't missed its mark of [Secretary of State] Seward's jugular? Or if after the assassination of Lincoln, all went to pieces and the presidential transition process fell prey to momentary passions and fears? Or if Joe Johnston had not decided to disobey Jefferson Davis's orders [and continued fighting]?

The Ugly Consequences of Revolution

To ask these questions, just a number of those faced by North and South at critical turning points in April, is to contemplate the answers—and in each case, the answers are terrible; the ugly consequences indeed incalculable. In Europe, by way of analogy, when the revolution in France finally quieted down, it could not be forgotten. Instead, it became lodged in the collective memory, a frightful, defining event with which each succeeding generation had to come to terms. Some lived in fear, others in hope that the giant was only sleeping and might be aroused. And aroused it was, as Europe felt the aftershocks of upheaval for the better part of a century to follow, a contagion of strife and conflict that swept across an entire continent, leaving a trail of tears and disorder.

Closer to home, other examples were no less heartening. At the turn of the nineteenth century, civil war in South and Central America, the other America, had slid into guerrilla war, the two becoming so intermingled that the wars between the rebels and Spain and between pro- and anti-royalist elements literally dragged on for decades. The effect was terrible: it hindered the rule of law and the development of stable democracy, and it devolved into Caesarism, military rule, army mutinies and revolts, and, as scholars ruefully note, every kind of barbaric cruelty. The suffering and bitterness that it engendered led to ongoing revolutionary struggles and profound weaknesses and instability in the independent civil and political societies that arose from it, lasting in one shape or form to this very day.

So, after April 1865, when the blood had clotted and dried, when the cadavers had been removed and the graves filled in, what America was asking for, at the war's end, was in fact something quite unique: a special exemption from the cruel edicts of history.

A New Mood in America

But that is largely what happened. By April's end, the country had been changed. Amid the wreckage of war, a kind of universal joint had been shifted, creating one of those rare seismic jolts that history rarely notes more than once a century or even once a millennium. Slowly across the land, in the North as well as the South, a powerful new mood was rising, which would alter the great stream of American—and hence, world—events. In no small measure, this was due, as we have seen, to the actions of a handful of leaders, Union as well as Confederate. And in a way, it calls to mind another pivotal era. Inspired by fifteenth-century Florence, the French sought to capture the awakening of the human spirit and combined the verb *renaître*, "revive," with the feminine noun *naissance*, "birth," to form Renaissance—rebirth. This, too, was a kind of rebirth and was equally compelling; but this new beginning was also something quite different. One ingredient that had heretofore been missing in American life would now emerge, phoenixlike, out of the war's ashes.

"It seems as if we were never alive until now," one New York woman had exulted after Fort Sumter, "never had a country till now." But never was this more true than, paradoxically, in the latticed gloom of the war's end. Walt Whitman said it well: "Strange, (is it not?) that battle, martyrs, blood, even assassination should so condense—perhaps only really, lastingly condense—a Nationality." So did the newly constituted periodical *The Nation*, which wrote, "The measure of the nation is now ratified by the blood of thousands of her sons." And now, remarkably, perhaps bafflingly, that nation at long last included the South—the South, which was unique and separate *before* the war began; the South, which had been literally turned upside down by its Northern enemies; the South, which had seen almost all that it loved and cherished wrecked and ruined. But there it was. "Strange as it may seem," observed T. Morris Chester, the black correspondent filing his vivid April and May 1865 dispatches from Richmond, "the better class of Southern People generally are of the opinion, and I think they are sincere, that the government and the union are now stronger today than ever before . . . [and] with great unanimity agree that slavery and rebellion are both consigned to one grave." And he added this stunning note: "All classes of persons . . ." he wrote, "have announced with a great deal of unanimity, that they were heartily rejoiced to be back in the old Union again of a grand and great country; many of them rebels from the beginning."

A Break with the Past

In truth, more than the Confederacy was vanquished by war's end. This is a subtle point but crucial to understand. In a profound but real sense, the chain of history had been irrevocably broken, for also destroyed was the Union, which would soon become little more than a distant, quaint, outdated concept. Regionalism would always be a factor in American life. But obliterated was any serious thought of future secession, by any side, any state, any section. Before the war, Americans often spoke of the United States in the plural—"The United States are . . ." For example, in his classic work on the history of America, noted historian John H. Hinton wrote in 1834: "By some, the United States are highly eulogized; by others, they are eagerly depreciated." Sometime after the war, however, so changed was America that this was now modified to a singular noun. Thus, Hinton's words would become, "The United States is . . ." The war's end—and how it ended, both manner and means—had, in fact, marked a decisive break with the past, the great chasm between the era of contingent republics and permanent nations, which until then was all of human doings. No less than the Founders who assembled in 1776, it made America.

Of course, this was not sudden. The process had, in one form or another, been under way before the war began. In a sense, the concept of secession had already been heatedly contested. Centrifugal change had been moving fervently apace for decades, hastened by the fervent push-pull of American migration westward and European emigration eastward; by the stunning emergence of industrial capitalism and by a bountiful economy; by new horizons created by the rising expansion of education and literacy and by the dazzling information and transportation revolutions that knit together a growing landmass; and by the astonishing growth of a nascent phenomenon that would come to be known as the "middle class." All these forces suggested unity, discredited disharmony, loosened the allure of sectionalism and secession, and strengthened the appeal of nationalism. Yet in the end, they would have been largely moot had the war—and had the days of April—gone differently. In the midst of all this ferment, anything could still have happened. Instead, April was that magic moment when these ideas joined together. Amid the long lists of heroic and historic actions for this country, April 1865 was incontestably one of America's finest hours: for it was not the deranged spirit of an assassin that defined the country at war's end, but the conciliatory spirit of leaders who led as much in peace as in war, warriors and politicians who, by their example, their exhortation, and their deeds, overcame their personal rancor, their heartache, and spoke as citizens of not two lands, but one, thereby bringing the country together. True, much hard work remained. But much, too, had already been accomplished.

And thus, by the war's end, this, too, was surely the case: the states alone were no longer America, and America was no longer simply states. Gone forever was the talk of replicating other civilizations—a new Rome or a new Athens, even a new London.

That was the meaning of April 1865. . . .

America would now be something different, not simply a clever political arrangement but a transcendent and pervading idea; it would be a new America, reunited, yes, scarred, certainly, but for the first time, largely whole, looking as much to the future as to the past. For some 135 years afterward, it would remain a diverse and democratic country, inspiring quests for freedom around the globe. And that same global stage, all too often riddled with malignant hatreds and civil strife, would remind us that it did not have to be this way. However successful or pervasive, an idea can be replaced, altered, modified, ignored. It could still be today; complacency should never allow one to think otherwise. As Lincoln understood most poignantly, it is not merely how arms are taken up, and why, but equally how they are laid back down, and why. And what then follows.

Democracy Was the Victor in the Civil War

James A. Rawley

In *Turning Points of the Civil War*, historian James A. Raw-ley examines key events in the conflict that turned the tide of the war: the South's early victories, the North's victory at Antietam, the issuance of the Emancipation Proclama-tion, and the Battle of Gettysburg. In the afterword to that text, Rawley summarizes the changes wrought upon the United States by the Civil War. He concludes that the war, above all else, resulted in a victory for American democracy. In Rawley's view, the Civil War was "mitigated tragedy" because it perpetuated America's democratic ex-periment by upholding majority rule, freeing 4 million slaves, and strengthening the U.S. Constitution by ex-tending the civil rights of African American citizens.

The Civil War was a major turning point in United States history. From the beginning of the Republic to the end of isolation, with the Second World War, there is no higher watershed than the decision of Appomattox. The vindication of American nationality was meaningful, primarily for polit-ical democracy and human equality, but its effects stretched out in many other directions.

The price of victory, human and material, was vast. The war's imprint on the American economy deeply stamped its future. The American Constitution was substantially re-vised by amendment and interpretation. The structure of American political parties today, particularly in the South, is a legacy of the war; and the South retains a separate iden-tity largely because of the war. American literature is richer, the study of military history profounder, the pantheon of heroes larger, the American presidency stronger as a result of the conflict.

A Victory for Democracy

What the success of the American experiment denoted for democracy, at home and abroad, was best voiced by Lincoln at Gettysburg when he dedicated his generation to the resolution "that this nation, under God, shall have a new birth of freedom—and that government of the people, by the people, for the people, shall not perish from the earth." The vindication of majority rule gave a new dimension to the meaning of the word democracy.

European liberals hailed the triumph of democratic principles in the United States. English workingmen, struggling for the franchise, turned the victory to their advantage. "Our opponents told us that Republicanism was on its trial," declared an English liberal newspaper in April, 1865. "They may rely upon it that a vast impetus has been given to Republican sentiments in England, and that they will have to reckon with it before long." The Reform Bill of 1867 was the fruition of a British movement that had been quickened by American developments.

The playwright Ibsen saw in the war's outcome a challenge to conservative Europe:

Thou Europe old, with order and law,
  With maxims that never fail,
With an unstained name, without blemish or flaw,
  With a virtue that keeps all meanness in awe,
Why grew'st thou so strangely pale?

And the Italian patriot and republican, Mazzini, paid homage to America: "You have done more for us in four years than fifty years of teaching, preaching, and writing from all your European brothers have been able to do."

In international affairs, the American democracy—reunited—was able at once to confront the French threat in Mexico to the Monroe Doctrine by sending about 50,000 troops to the Texas border. Under a variety of pressures, among them American military might, Napoleon III ultimately withdrew, removing the threefold threat to our national security and prestige of French influence in Mexico, of a Mexican monarchy, and of possible expansion in the New World. A century of Anglo-American hostility passed into eclipse with the settlement of the *Alabama* claims in 1872, and a new century of Anglo-American friendship dawned; today the Anglo-American *entente* is the firmest bastion of American foreign policy. The might of the United States in two world wars, in partnership with Britain, has perpetuated freedom in the Western world. A United States divided at the Potomac would doubtless have been less equal to the international challenges of the twentieth century.

The War Freed Four Million Slaves

Second in impressiveness only to the preserving of the American polity and the principles it lived by was the freeing of four million human beings by the brute force of war. By 1861, slavery was an anachronism in the Western world—its existence in the United States had violated the whole tenor of the American experiment. Not only had liberty and equality been denied the blacks, but slavery had fettered the freedom of whites, North and South. The war inadvertently broke a log jam, and a movement long-delayed gave freedom to the millions. Few events in nineteenth-century American history can rival in importance the abolition of human bondage. However, we must note, the violence of the context of emancipation and the abruptness of the act failed to secure civil liberties and equality to the freedmen. Nonetheless, the doctrine of equality passed beyond old bounds of American democratic thought during the Civil War.

The Costs and Consequences of War

The cost in human lives exceeded that of any other American war. National unity was purchased at a price of 617,000 lives—a figure that overtowers the 112,000 American fatalities of World War I and the 322,000 of World War II. The incidence of 258,000 fatalities among the 5,500,000 people of the South bore heavily upon this region that lost so great a proportion of young men—the flower of the Confederacy, the seedcorn of its future.

The material cost to the nation was five billion dollars, to the South inestimable. Southern destitution after the war is embedded in Southern tradition. Long swaths of land lay devastated by marching and countermarching armies. Houses, buildings, fences, and railways had been torn down, or stood neglected. Fortunes had been obliterated, social classes dissolved, political leaders proscribed, the gentry disfranchised.

All this is true, or nearly enough true, not to warrant a quibble. But what is arresting is the South's loss of economic eminence. If cotton had been king before the war, steel, oil, wheat, and meat wielded the scepter in the new generation. Though one can demonstrate the recovery and growth of the cotton growing and cotton spinning South in the decades immediately after Appomattox, the general picture is one of regional retardation in a nation being transformed by industrialization. Notwithstanding the presence of abundant resources, Southerners long continued to subsist on an inadequate living standard, as the Federal government's *Report on Economic Conditions of the South* pointed out in 1938. In that year President Franklin D. Roosevelt declared: "It is my conviction that the South presents right now the nation's No. 1 economic problem." And, for a generation or more after the war, the whole nation bore an onerous burden of taxes to redeem war bonds and to rescue veterans from penury and defecting from the Republican party.

The war transformed American economic institutions. The United States maintained its policy of protectionism for two generations; not until 1913 did the nation scale down its tariff wall to a moderate height. The printing of greenbacks to finance the war nurtured debtors' dreams of easy escape from creditors throughout the panics and depressions of succeeding epochs. The nation reorganized its banking institutions during the war by establishing a system of national banks, creating a new kind of national money, and terminating the chaotic issue of notes by state banks. The Federal government used the public domain to promote homesteading, transcontinental railroads, and agricultural and mechanical colleges. Contrary to what is usually said, the war may well have retarded industrialization instead of accelerated it. Analysis of statistical series indicates economic growth, which had been advancing very rapidly before the war, sank to a low level in the sixties.

Amending the Constitution

As a result of the war the American Constitution was amended, both in body and spirit. Three amendments ended slavery, extended citizenship to Negroes, and banned denial of the right to vote on account of race, color, or previous condition of servitude. Collectively, the amendments disinherited the states of traditional rights. The victory of American nationalism won its classic formulation in 1869 in the decision of *Texas* v. *White*, when the Supreme Court repudiated the secession theory and ruled that "the Constitution . . . looks to an indestructible Union, composed of indestructible States."

In astounding acts of judicial legerdemain, the Court subsequently withdrew privileges of the Fourteenth Amendment from Negroes, conferred them on corporations, denied them to labor unions, and guaranteed the *Federal* Bill of Rights against *state* encroachment. Only in recent years has the Court sought to restore the amendment to its pristine meaning. Grave as were the abuses made by a false construction of the Fourteenth Amendment, the nation had made a Constitutional commitment to human equality, which is tortuously being realized in the second half of the twentieth century.

A Republican Victory

In the realm of party politics, the Civil War was a vital issue through the period of Republican ascendancy, into the time of William McKinley—the last Civil War veteran to serve as president. The Democratic party wore the taint of Copperheadism, the Republican party brandished the bloody shirt, and the GAR gave its votes for Republicans and pensions; in the campaign of 1884 a partisan smeared the Democrats as the party of "Rum, Romanism, and Rebellion." The "Confederacy" maintained itself as the "Solid South"; it disenfranchised the Negro, entrenched itself on congressional committees through the seniority system, and continued for a century after the cessation of hostilities, to keep a watch on the Potomac.

Defeated, humiliated, impoverished, and reduced in political influence, the South suffered a psychic scar—perhaps the most intangible but most enduring outcome of the war for white Southerners. If Southern nationalism was defeated at Appomattox, it rose again from the ashes of Reconstruction. Ambivalent between the Old and the New South, the section adjusted its labor system to a new form of peonage in share-cropping and mill towns, pursued Northern industry but eschewed trade unionism, fought in American wars but continued to sing "Dixie," accepted Federal funds but preached state rights, claimed power in the councils of the Democratic party but organized a Dixiecrat revolt. Whatever their vagaries of behavior, Southerners remained keenly conscious of themselves as Southerners, sensitive to external criticism, and unable to laugh at themselves.

A Subject for Writers and Historians

Southern agrarians defiantly offered their manifesto in the book, *I'll Take My Stand* in 1930. Margaret Mitchell's *Gone with the Wind* resoundingly resurrected, in 1936, a romantic past for delighted Southerners. The so-called Southern Renaissance of literature, absorbed in Southern themes, was a latter-day witness of the stamp made by the Civil War upon *belles-lettres* and upon historical writing. In earlier generations, Mary Johnston and Ellen Glasgow had drawn inspiration from the war and its aftermath.

The Civil War has been an endless battlefield for students of military history. Its strategy and tactics formed textbook lessons at West Point, Annapolis, and Sandhurst. The generalship of Lee, Jackson, Grant, Sherman, and others influenced later generations of soldiers. The military use of railroads, entrenchments, the conception of total war, the method of conscription—all provided matter for deliberation in Western nations. The United States drew bountifully on its Civil War experience in organizing for the First World War. A war of sabres and ironclad ships, the Civil War was the last of the romantic and the first of the modern wars.

The Presidency Strengthened

The Civil War broadened the American presidency. The office had been limited by the Constitution and tradition before Lincoln's accession to it. Only one president, Andrew Jackson, had construed his powers in a nationalistic and popular sense; and he had provoked an anti-executive opposition that took the name Whig party, in remembrance of opponents of Stuart tyranny. Lincoln discovered a new source of national authority: the war power claimed by the executive, and he inaugurated war, proclaimed a blockade, raised an army, suspended the writ of *habeas corpus*, and spent Federal funds—all without authorization by Congress. His issuance of the Emancipation Proclamation flaunted the presidential prerogative in a manner without parallel in American history, invading the rights of the states, and confiscating billions of dollars. True, presidential power subsequently deteriorated under the congressional assault on Andrew Johnson and his successors, but Lincoln's legacy to Theodore Roosevelt, Woodrow Wilson, Franklin Roosevelt, and others was a vigorous executive, identified with the popular interest.

The war lengthened the gallery of national heroes. Lincoln became, in popular esteem, one of the greatest American presidents. The Confederate general, Robert E. Lee, was transfigured into a national hero, second only to George Washington in perfection of character. U. S. Grant was celebrated as the warrior who saved the Union, and was twice rewarded with the presidency. The dour and indomitable Stonewall Jackson perhaps stands unrivaled for the brilliance of his tactics. A host of lesser men in blue and gray—among them Sherman, Thomas, Stuart, Forrest—occupy conspicuous pedestals.

A Mitigated Tragedy

The Civil War was America's tragedy. It was a tragic failure of the democratic process, of national statesmanship, of Constitutional government. Compromise and reason receded in the face of rigidity and passion. Fellow citizens went to war and killed one another by the hundreds of thousands. Property was expropriated by the hundreds of millions. The black race was freed, exalted, and then abandoned.

Yet the Civil War, once thrust upon the Republic, was a mitigated tragedy. It perpetuated the American nation, the democratic experiment, and Constitutional government. It extinguished human slavery in the United States of America. Nationalism, democracy, and constitutionalism preserved—and freedom gained—are no mean heritage of a war.

In 1865 the United States turned away from state sovereignty, minority rule, secessionism, and slavery. It faced the future.

The Civil War Caused a National Power Shift

James M. McPherson

James M. McPherson, the noted Civil War historian who teaches at Princeton University, won the Pulitzer Prize for *Battle Cry of Freedom: The Civil War Era*. He has also authored *Marching Toward Freedom: The Negro in the Civil War, Ordeal by Fire: The Civil War and Reconstruction*, and several other important studies of the Civil War era. In this excerpt from the epilogue of *Battle Cry of Freedom*, McPherson identifies one of the important consequences wrought by the Civil War—a shift in political power from South to North. According to McPherson, the war destroyed the South's vision of America and made the North's vision the vision for the nation as it headed into the twentieth century. In that sense, the Civil War permanently changed the face and direction of America.

Arguments about the causes and consequences of the Civil War, as well as the reasons for northern victory, will continue as long as there are historians to wield the pen—which is, perhaps even for this bloody conflict, mightier than the sword. But certain large consequences of the war seem clear. Secession and slavery were killed, never to be revived during the century and a quarter since Appomattox. These results signified a broader transformation of American society and polity punctuated if not alone achieved by the war. Before 1861 the two words "United States" were generally rendered as a plural noun: "the United States *are* a republic." The war marked a transition of the United States to a singular noun. The "Union" also became the nation, and Americans now rarely speak of their Union except in an historical sense. Lincoln's wartime speeches betokened this transition. In his first inaugural address he used the word "Union" twenty times and the word "nation" not once. In his first message to Congress, on July 4, 1861, he used "Union" thirty-two times and "nation" three times. In his letter to Horace Greeley of August 22, 1862, on the relationship of slavery to the war, Lincoln spoke of the Union eight times and of the nation not at all. Little more than a year later, in his address at Gettysburg, the president did not refer to the "Union" at all but used the word "nation" five times to invoke a new birth of freedom and nationalism for the United States. And in his second inaugural address, looking back over the events of the past four years, Lincoln spoke of one side seeking to dissolve the *Union* in 1861 and the other accepting the challenge of war to preserve the *nation.*

A Centralized Government Dominated by the North

The old federal republic in which the national government had rarely touched the average citizen except through the post-office gave way to a more centralized polity that taxed the people directly and created an internal revenue bureau to collect these taxes, drafted men into the army, expanded the jurisdiction of federal courts, created a national currency and a national banking system, and established the first national agency for social welfare—the Freedmen's Bureau. Eleven of the first twelve amendments to the Constitution had limited the powers of the national government; six of the next seven, beginning with the Thirteenth Amendment in 1865, vastly expanded those powers at the expense of the states.

This change in the federal balance paralleled a radical shift of political power from South to North. During the first seventy-two years of the republic down to 1861 a slaveholding resident of one of the states that joined the Confederacy had been President of the United States for forty-nine of those years—more than two-thirds of the time. In Congress, twenty-three of the thirty-six speakers of the House and twenty-four of the presidents pro tem of the Senate had been

southerners. The Supreme Court always had a southern majority; twenty of the thirty-five justices to 1861 had been appointed from slave states. After the war a century passed before a resident of an ex-Confederate state was elected
president. For half a century *none* of the speakers of the
House or presidents pro tem of the Senate came from the
South, and only five of the twenty-six Supreme Court justices
appointed during that half-century were southerners.

These figures symbolize a sharp and permanent change in
the direction of American development. Through most of
American history the South has seemed different from the
rest of the United States, with "a separate and unique iden-
tity . . . which appeared to be out of the mainstream of American experience." But when did the northern stream become
the mainstream? From a broader perspective it may have
been the *North* that was exceptional and unique before the
Civil War. The South more closely resembled a majority of
the societies in the world than did the rapidly changing
North during the antebellum generation. Despite the abolition of legal slavery or serfdom throughout much of the western hemisphere and western Europe, most of the world—like
the South—had an unfree or quasi-free labor force. Most societies in the world remained predominantly rural, agricultural, and labor-intensive; most, including even several European countries, had illiteracy rates as high or higher than the
South's 45 percent; most like the South remained bound by
traditional values and networks of family, kinship, hierarchy,
and patriarchy. The North—along with a few countries of
northwestern Europe—hurtled forward eagerly toward a future of industrial capitalism that many southerners found dis-
tasteful if not frightening; the South remained proudly and
even defiantly rooted in the past before 1861.

The South's Vision of America Destroyed

Thus when secessionists protested that they were acting to
preserve traditional rights and values, they were correct.
They fought to protect their constitutional liberties against
the perceived northern threat to overthrow them. The
South's concept of republicanism had not changed in three-

quarters of a century; the North's had. With complete sincerity the South fought to preserve its version of the republic of the founding fathers—a government of limited powers that protected the rights of property and whose constituency comprised an independent gentry and yeomanry of the white race undisturbed by large cities, heartless factories, restless free workers, and class conflict. The accession to power of the Republican party, with its ideology of competitive, egalitarian, free-labor capitalism, was a signal to the South that the northern majority had turned irrevocably toward this frightening, revolutionary future. Indeed, the Black Republican party appeared to the eyes of many southerners as "essentially a revolutionary party" composed of "a motley throng of Sans culottes . . . Infidels and freelovers, interspersed by Bloomer women, fugitive slaves, and amalgamationists." Therefore secession was a pre-emptive counterrevolution to prevent the Black Republican revolution from engulfing the South. "We are not revolutionists," insisted James B.D. DeBow and Jefferson Davis during the Civil War, "We are resisting revolution. . . . We are conservative."

Union victory in the war destroyed the southern vision of America and ensured that the northern vision would become the American vision. Until 1861, however, it was the North that was out of the mainstream, not the South. Of course the northern states, along with Britain and a few countries in northwestern Europe, were cutting a new channel in world history that would doubtless have become the mainstream even if the American Civil War had not happened. Russia had abolished serfdom in 1861 to complete the dissolution of this ancient institution of bound labor in Europe. But for Americans the Civil War marked the turning point. A Louisiana planter who returned home sadly after the war wrote in 1865: "Society has been completely changed by the war. The [French] revolution of '89 did not produce a greater change in the 'Ancien Régime' than this has in our social life." And four years later George Ticknor, a retired Harvard professor, concluded that the Civil War had created a "great gulf between what happened before in our century and what has happened since, or what is likely to happen hereafter. It does not seem to me as if I were living in the country in which I was born." From the war sprang the great flood that caused the stream of American history to surge into a new channel and transferred the burden of exceptionalism from North to South.

What would be the place of freed slaves and their descendants in this new order? In 1865 a black soldier who recognized his former master among a group of Confederate prisoners he was guarding called out a greeting: "Hello, massa; bottom rail on top dis time!"

The Civil War Prompted the Development of Big Technology and Big Business

Robert Penn Warren

During the twentieth century, Robert Penn Warren, a native of Kentucky, emerged as one of the South's most distinguished men of letters. He won Pulitzer Prizes for both fiction and poetry and also authored essays and nonfiction books, including *Segregation: The Inner Conflict in the South*. To commemorate the one hundredth anniversary of the start of the Civil War, Warren wrote *The Legacy of the Civil War: Meditations on the Centennial*. In this excerpt from that text, Warren discusses one important effect of the Civil War—the stimulation of technology and big business. In Warren's view, the war changed the United States from "an agrarian, handicraft society into the society of Big Technology and Big Business."

The new nation came not merely from a military victory. It came from many circumstances created or intensified by the War. The War enormously stimulated technology and productivity. Actually, it catapulted America from what had been in considerable part an agrarian, handicraft society into the society of Big Technology and Big Business. "Parallel with the waste and sorrows of war," as [historian] Allan Nevins puts it, "ran a stimulation of individual initiative, a challenge to large-scale planning, and an encouragement of co-operative effort, which in combination with new agencies for developing natural resources amounted to a great release of creative energy." The old sprawling, loosely knit country disappeared into the nation of Big Organization.

Robert Penn Warren, *The Legacy of the Civil War: Meditations on the Centennial*. New York: Random House, 1961.

The War Spurred Inventions and Creativity

It is true that historians can debate the question whether, in the long run and in the long perspective, war—even wars of that old pre-atomic age—can stimulate creativity and production. And it is true that there had been a surge of technological development in the decade or so before 1861, followed, some maintain, by an actual decline in inventiveness during the War. But the question is not how many new inventions were made but how the existing ones were used. The little device of the "jig," which, back in 1798, had enabled Eli Whitney to make firearms with interchangeable parts led now to the great mass-production factories of the Civil War—factories used not merely for firearms but for all sorts of products. The Civil War demanded the great American industrial plant, and the industrial plant changed American society.

To take one trivial fact, the ready-made clothing industry was an offshoot of the mass production of blue uniforms—and would not this standardization of fashion, after the sartorial whim, confusion, fantasy and individualism of an earlier time, have some effect on man's relation to man? But to leap from the trivial to the grand, the War prepared the way for the winning of the West. Before the War a transcontinental railroad was already being planned, and execution was being delayed primarily by debate about the route to take, a debate which in itself sprang from, and contributed something to, the intersectional acrimony. After the War, debate did not long delay action. But the War did more than remove impediment to this scheme. It released enormous energies, new drives and know-how for the sudden and massive occupation of the continent. And for the great adventure there was a new cutting edge of profit.

The Economic Consequences of the War

Not only the industrial plant but the economic context in which industry could thrive came out of the War. The Morril tariff of 1861 actually preceded the firing on Sumter, but it was the mark of Republican victory and an omen of what was to come; and no session of Congress for the next four

Total War

According to Civil War historian James M. McPherson, the Civil War introduced the United States to the concept of "total war," defined as a devastating conflict that mobilizes the entire population in the war effort.

The Civil War mobilized human resources on a scale unmatched by any other event in American history except, perhaps, World War II. For actual combat duty the Civil War mustered a considerably larger proportion of American manpower than did World War II. And, in another comparison with that global conflict, the victorious power in the Civil War did all it could to devastate the enemy's economic resources as well as the morale of its home-front population, which was considered almost as important as enemy armies in the war effort. In World War II this was done by strategic bombing; in the Civil War it was done by cavalry and infantry penetrating deep into the Confederate heartland.

It is these factors—the devastation wrought by the war, the radical changes it accomplished, and the mobilization of the whole society to sustain the war effort—that have caused many historians to label the Civil War as a "total war."

James M. McPherson, *Drawn With the Sword: Reflections on the American Civil War.* New York: Oxford University Press, 1996, p. 67.

years failed to raise the tariff. Even more importantly came the establishment of a national banking system in place of the patchwork of state banks, and the issuing of national greenbacks to rationalize the crazy currency system of the state-bank notes. The new system, plus government subsidy, honed the cutting edge of profit. "The fact is that people have the money and they are looking around to see what to do with it," said the New York magnate William E. Dodge in a speech in Baltimore in 1865. At last, he said, there was indigenous capital to "develop the natural interests of the country." And he added, enraptured: "The mind staggers as we begin to contemplate the future."

The mind staggered, and the bookkeeping in New York

by the new breed of businessmen fostered by the Civil War was as potent a control for the centrifugal impulses of the South and West as ever bayonet or railroad track. The pen, if not mightier than the sword, was very effective in consolidating what the sword had won—when the pen was wielded by the bookkeeper.

Not only New York bookkeeping but Washington bookkeeping was a new force for union. The war had cost money. Hamilton's dream of a national debt to insure national stability was realized, by issuing the bonds so efficiently peddled by Jay Cooke, to a degree astronomically beyond [Alexander] Hamilton's rosiest expectations. For one thing, this debt meant a new tax relation of the citizen to the Federal government, including the new income tax; the citizen had a new and poignant sense of the reality of Washington. But the great hand that took could also give, and with pensions and subsidies, the iron dome of the Capitol took on a new luster in the eyes of millions of citizens.

Soldiers Saw the Country

Furthermore, the War meant that Americans saw America. The farm boy of Ohio, the trapper of Minnesota, and the pimp of the Mackerelville section of New York City saw Richmond and Mobile. They not only saw America, they saw each other, and together shot it out with some Scot of the Valley of Virginia or ducked hardware hurled by a Louisiana Jew who might be a lieutenant of artillery, CSA [Confederate States of America]. By the War, not only Virginia and Louisiana were claimed for the union. Ohio and Minnesota were, in fact, claimed too—claimed so effectively that for generations the memory of the Bloody Shirt and the GAR [Grand Army of the Republic] would prompt many a Middlewestern farmer to vote almost automatically against his own interests.

Discussion Questions

Chapter 1: A Nation Divides: The Causes of the Civil War

1. At least three of the viewpoints in Chapter 1 identify slavery as a direct or indirect cause of the Civil War. Would the war have occurred if the South had, during the 1850s, gradually decided to abolish slavery? Were the other differences between North and South cited in the Chapter 1 viewpoints substantial enough to ignite a civil war between North and South?

2. Patrick Gerster and Nicholas Cords point out that Northern and Southern historians have offered significantly different explanations for the causes of the Civil War. Summarize the views of the Northern and Southern historians, and explain why the two groups might come to different conclusions.

3. Don E. Fehrenbacher points to the election of Abraham Lincoln as the event that pushed several Southern states to secession. Why would the election of Lincoln be so problematic for the South?

4. According to D.W. Meinig, what geographical issues pushed the North and South toward civil war in 1861?

5. Bruce Catton describes the differences between the North and the South in terms of the differences between Robert E. Lee and Ulysses S. Grant. Is it fair to use a single individual from each region to represent the region? Were there men like Lee in the North and men like Grant in the South?

Chapter 2: Early Battlefield Victories and the Prospect of European Intervention Fuel the South's Hope for Independence

1. The viewpoints in this chapter suggest that for almost two years the South was winning the Civil War. What would the South have needed to do to retain its advantage?

2. Joseph L. Harsh explains that Confederate president Jefferson Davis designed an "offensive-defensive" strategy for winning the war. What does Harsh mean by that term, and how might such a strategy have helped the South to victory?

3. Geoffrey C. Ward, Ric Burns, and Ken Burns describe the con-

vincing Confederate victory in the Battle of Bull Run, the first major engagement of the Civil War. Why was it important for the South to win that battle? If the Union had won that battle, would the war have lasted only one or two years instead of four years?

4. According to Howard Jones, the Confederacy worked hard to gain official recognition from Great Britain and France. Why was foreign recognition so vital to the South's cause?

5. The Union's devastating defeat at the Battle of Fredericksburg in December 1862 spread pessimism throughout the North. Why was that defeat particularly troubling for Northerners? Why would the battle so raise the South's hopes for victory and independence?

Chapter 3: The North Gains the Advantage

1. Battlefield victories at Antietam, Gettysburg, and Vicksburg helped change the tide of the war in the North's favor. But the authors of the viewpoints in Chapter 3 suggest other factors that contributed to the North's gaining the advantage. What other political or military decisions propelled the North to victory?

2. Discuss the military, political, and diplomatic consequences of the battle of Antietam, as presented by James M. McPherson.

3. William L. Barney suggests that President Abraham Lincoln's decision, in 1863, to allow African Americans to join the Union army was a turning point in the war. Why were African Americans prohibited from joining the armed forces before 1863?

4. How did President Lincoln's issuance of the Emancipation Proclamation redefine the purpose of the Civil War?

5. According to James R. Arnold, why was the Union victory at the Battle of Vicksburg so important? What might have happened if General Grant had been defeated at Vicksburg?

6. According to T. Harry Williams, what qualities made Ulysses S. Grant a superior general?

7. Phillip Shaw Paludan offers several factors that contributed to the North's victory in the Civil War. Which factor is the most compelling? Given the North's economic and manpower advantages, could the South have won the war?

Chapter 4: A Changed Nation

1. All of the viewpoints in Chapter 4 discuss changes wrought in the United States by the Civil War. What changes might not have occurred if the South had won? How would the nation be different today if the South had won the war?

2. According to Jay Winik, political and military leaders of the victorious North and the defeated South collaborated to re-establish the United States as a single democratic nation in the aftermath of the Civil War. What steps did these leaders take to ensure national unity in the wake of such a bitter and devastating conflict? If these leaders had taken a different course—for example, if General Robert E. Lee had continued to fight rather than surrender at Appomattox—how would the postwar years have differed?

3. James A. Rawley argues that the Civil War was a "mitigated tragedy." What does he mean? What factors mitigated the devastation caused by the Civil War?

4. According to James M. McPherson, the Civil War destroyed the South's vision for the United States. What was the South's vision for the nation, and why did the war destroy it?

5. Robert Penn Warren suggests that the Civil War resulted in the development of Big Technology and Big Business. How did the war stimulate business and technological development?

Appendix of Documents

Document 1: The Declaration of Independence

The Declaration of Independence, made public on July 4, 1776, an-
nounces to the world that Great Britain's American colonies are free from
their mother country's rule. The document identifies the newly free
colonies as both united colonies and free and independent states. The doc-
ument also asserts that all men are created equal, a clause contradicted by
the institution of slavery.

We hold these truths to be self-evident: That all men are created
equal; that they are endowed by their Creator with certain un-
alienable rights; that among these are life, liberty, and the pursuit
of happiness; that, to secure these rights, governments are instituted among men, deriving their just powers from the consent of
the governed. . . .

We, therefore, the representatives of the United States of America, in General Congress assembled, appealing to the Supreme
Judge of the world for the rectitude of our intentions, do, in the
name and by the authority of the good people of these colonies,
solemnly publish and declare, that these United Colonies are, and
of right ought to be, FREE AND INDEPENDENT STATES;
that they are absolved from all allegiance to the British crown, and
that all political connection between them and the state of Great
Britain is, and ought to be, totally dissolved. . . .

The Declaration of Independence, 1776.

Document 2: The Ordinance of 1787

The first attempt by Congress to deal with the issue of slavery in United
States territories predates the ratification of the Constitution. In 1787,
Congress, operating under the Articles of Confederation, passed the Or-
dinance of 1787, which prohibited slavery in the United States territo-
ries northwest of the Ohio River.

There shall be neither slavery nor involuntary servitude in the said
Territory, otherwise than in punishment of crimes, whereof the
party shall have been duly convicted: Provided always, that any
person escaping into the same from whom labor or service is lawfully claimed in any one of the original States, such fugitive may be

lawfully reclaimed and conveyed to the person claiming his or her labor or service as aforesaid.

Quoted in Mason Lowance, *Against Slavery: An Abolitionist Reader.* New York: Penguin Books, 2000.

Document 3: The Constitution on Slavery

The United States Constitution, as drafted in 1787, did not include the words "slavery" or "slave," but it referred to slaves in two sections. Article I states that representation for each state in the House of Representatives will be determined by counting the number of free persons and adding to that sum "three-fifths of all other persons."

Representatives and direct taxes shall be apportioned among the several States which may be included within this Union, according to their respective numbers, *which shall be determined by adding to the whole number of free persons, including those bound to service for a term of years and excluding Indians not taxed, three-fifths of all other persons.*

Article IV of the Constitution mandates that escaped slaves will be returned to their owners.

No person held in service or labor in one State, under the laws thereof, escaping into another, shall, in consequence of any law or regulation therein, be discharged from such service or labor, but shall be delivered up on claim of the party to whom such service or labor may be due.

The United States Constitution, 1787.

Document 4: The Missouri Compromise

In 1820, Congress again attempted to deal with the issue of slavery in the United States territories by passing the Missouri Compromise, which admitted Missouri and Maine to the Union and included a stipulation prohibiting slavery north of the 36'30° latitude mark. The Missouri Compromise resolved a crisis in Congress between Northern and Southern legislators that began when Missouri applied to join the Union as a slave state. The United States Supreme Court's decision in the 1857 case of Dred Scott *declared the Missouri Compromise unconstitutional.*

And be it further enacted, That in all that territory ceded by France to the United States, under the name of Louisiana, which lies north of the thirty-six degrees, and thirty minutes north latitude, not included within the limits of the state contemplated by their act, slavery and involuntary servitude, otherwise than in the punishment of crimes, whereof the parties shall have been duly convicted, shall be, and is hereby, forever prohibited.

Quoted in Mason Lowance, *Against Slavery: An Abolitionist Reader.* New York: Penguin Books, 2000.

Document 5: *Walker's Appeal*

In 1829, David Walker, an African American freeman, published an antislavery pamphlet titled Walker's Appeal in Four Articles. *In his Appeal, Walker suggested that God would eventually destroy the United States because of the sin of slavery. Walker's pamphlet was one of a growing number of abolitionist documents published during the 1820s and 1830s.*

I tell you Americans! that unless you speedily alter your course, *you* and your Country are gone!!!!! For God Almighty will tear up the very face of the earth!!! . . . I hope that the Americans may hear, but I am afraid that they have done us so much injury, and are so firm in their belief that our Creator made us to be an inheritance to them forever, that their hearts will be hardened, so that their destruction may be sure. This language, perhaps, is too harsh for the American's delicate ears. But O Americans! Americans!! I warn you in the name of the Lord . . . to repent and reform, or you are ruined!!!

Quoted in Diane Ravitch, ed., *The American Reader: Words That Moved a Nation.* New York: HarperCollins, 1990.

Document 6: The *Liberator*

On January 1, 1831, William Lloyd Garrison, a Boston abolitionist editor, commenced publication of the Liberator, *which would become the most prominent antislavery newspaper in the United States. Below is an excerpt from the editorial in the paper's first issue.*

Assenting to the "self-evident truth" maintained in the American Declaration of Independence, "that all men are created equal and endowed by their Creator with certain inalienable rights—among which are life, liberty and the pursuit of happiness," I shall strenuously contend for the immediate enfranchisement of our slave population. . . .

   I am aware that many object to the severity of my language; but is there not cause for severity? I *will be* as harsh as truth, and as uncompromising as justice. On this subject I do not wish to think, or speak, or write, with moderation. No! No! . . . I am in earnest—I will not equivocate—I will not excuse—I will not retreat a single inch—AND I WILL BE HEARD. The apathy of the people is enough to make every statue leap from its pedestal, and to hasten the resurrection of the dead.

Quoted in Diane Ravitch, ed., *The American Reader: Words That Moved a Nation.* New York: HarperCollins, 1990.

Document 7: Southerners Respond to Abolitionist Appeals

Southerners did not stand by meekly while abolitionists attacked the institution of slavery. The following statement is an excerpt from a speech made in defense of slavery by South Carolina legislator George McDuffie in 1835. McDuffie claims that enslaving African Americans enacts the will of God.

No human institution, in my opinion, is more manifestly consistent with the will of God than domestic slavery, and no one of His ordinances is written in more legible characters than that which consigns the African race to this condition, as more conducive to their own happiness, than any other which they are susceptible. Whether we consult the sacred Scriptures or the lights of nature and reason, we shall find these truths as abundantly apparent as if written with a sunbeam in the heavens. Under both the Jewish and Christian dispensations of our religion, domestic slavery existed with the unequivocal sanction of its prophets, its apostles, and finally its great Author. The patriarchs themselves, those chosen instruments of God, were slaveholders. In fact, the divine sanction of this institution is so plainly written that "he who runs may read" it, and those overrighteous pretenders and Pharisees who affect to be scandalized by its existence among us would do well to inquire how much more nearly they walk in the ways of godliness than did Abraham, Isaac, and Jacob.

That the African Negro is destined by Providence to occupy this condition of servile dependence is not less manifest. It is marked on the face, stamped on the skin, and evinced by the intellectual inferiority and natural improvidence of this race. They have all the qualities that fit them for slaves, and not one of those that would fit them to be freemen.

Quoted in William Dudley, ed., *Slavery: Opposing Viewpoints.* San Diego: Greenhaven Press, 1992.

Document 8: The Wilmot Proviso

In 1847, during the Mexican War, Representative David Wilmot of Pennsylvania introduced a bill in the House of Representatives that would prohibit slavery in all newly acquired United States territories. The bill passed in the House of Representatives but was blocked by Southern senators in the Senate. The bitter debate over the Wilmot Proviso widened the rift between North and South that was developing during the 1830s and 1840s.

And be it further enacted, that there shall be neither slavery nor involuntary servitude in any Territory on the Continent of America, which shall hereafter be acquired by, or annexed to, the United States, except for crimes whereof the party shall have been duly convicted: Provided always, that any person escaping into such Territory, from whom labor or service is lawfully claimed, in any one of the United States, such fugitive may be lawfully reclaimed and conveyed out of said territory to the person claiming his or her labor or service.

Quoted in Mason Lowance, *Against Slavery: An Abolitionist Reader.* New York: Penguin Books, 2000.

Document 9: The Fugitive Slave Law

In 1850, as part of the Compromise of 1850, Congress enacted a strict Fugitive Slave Law to deal with runaway slaves. The new law angered abolitionists who helped escaped slaves en route to freedom in Canada. For abolitionists, one of the most troubling aspects of the Fugitive Slave Law was Section 7, which levied a fine and prison term on any citizen who assisted a runaway slave or hindered an individual reclaiming a runaway slave. The Fugitive Slave Law further escalated tensions between North and South.

Be it further enacted, That any person who shall knowingly and willingly obstruct, hinder, or prevent such claimant, his agent or attorney, or any other person or persons lawfully assisting him, her or them, from arresting such a fugitive from service or labor, either with or without process as aforesaid, or shall rescue or attempt to rescue such fugitive from service or labor from the custody of such claimant, his agent or attorney, or other person or persons lawfully assisting as aforesaid, when so arrested pursuant to the authority herein given, and declared, or shall aid, abet, or assist such person so owing service or labor as aforesaid, directly or indirectly, to escape such claimant, his agent or attorney, or other persons legally authorized as aforesaid; or shall harbor or conceal such fugitives so as to prevent the discovery and arrest of such person, after notice or knowledge of the fact that such person was a fugitive from service or labor as aforesaid, shall, for either of said offences, be subject to a fine not exceeding one thousand dollars, and imprisonment not exceeding six months, by indictment and conviction before the District Court of the United States. . . .

Quoted in Mason Lowance, *Against Slavery: An Abolitionist Reader.* New York: Penguin Books, 2000.

Document 10: *Uncle Tom's Cabin*

In 1852, Harriet Beecher Stowe published the novel Uncle Tom's Cabin, *the most effective piece of abolitionist writing published in the United States. Stowe concluded her novel with a stern warning to North and South that some punishment from God would come upon the nation if it did not eliminate slavery, which Stowe considered a grave national sin. President Abraham Lincoln once reportedly referred to Stowe as "the little woman who wrote the book that started this great war."*

Are not these dread words for a nation bearing in her bosom so mighty an injustice? Christians! Every time that you pray that the kingdom of Christ may come, can you forget that prophecy associates, in dread fellowship, the *day of vengeance* with the year of His redeemed?

A day of grace is yet held out to us. Both North and South have been guilty before God; and the *Christian church* has a heavy account to answer. Not by combining together, to protect injustice and cruelty, and making a common capital of sin, is this Union to be saved,—but by repentance, justice, and mercy; for, not surer is the eternal law by which the millstone sinks in the ocean, than that stronger law, by which injustice and cruelty shall bring on nations the wrath of Almighty God!

Harriet Beecher Stowe, *Uncle Tom's Cabin*, 1852; reprint, New York: Bantam Books, 1981.

Document 11: The *Dred Scott* Decision

In 1857, the United States Supreme Court decided the fate of a slave named Dred Scott. Scott's master had taken him to reside for a time in the free territory of Minnesota and the free state of Illinois. When Scott's master died, Scott sued for his freedom, arguing that he had become a free man when he lived in a territory that prohibited slavery. Scott lost his case. In this excerpt from the Court's decision, Chief Justice Roger Taney explains that Scott, a slave, must be treated under law as a piece of property. The decision also negates the Missouri Compromise because an act of Congress cannot deny an American citizen's property rights.

The right of property in a slave is distinctly and expressly affirmed in the Constitution. The right to traffic in it, like an ordinary article of merchandise and property, was guaranteed to the citizens of the United States, in every State that might desire it, for twenty years. And the Government in express terms is pledged to protect it in all future time, if the slave escapes from his owner. This is done in plain words—too plain to be misunderstood. And no word can be found in the Constitution which gives Congress a greater power over slave property, or which entitles property of that kind to less protection than property of any other description. The only power conferred is the power coupled with the duty of guarding and protecting the owner in his rights.

Upon these considerations, it is the opinion of the court that the act of Congress which prohibited a citizen from holding and owning property of this kind in the territory of the United States north of the line therein mentioned, is not warranted by the Constitution, and is therefore void; and that neither Dred Scott himself, nor any of his family, were made free by being carried into this territory; even if they had been carried there by the owner, with the intention of becoming a permanent resident.

Quoted in William Dudley, ed., *Slavery: Opposing Viewpoints.* San Diego: Greenhaven Press, 1992.

Document 12: Abraham Lincoln's "House Divided" Speech

To kick off his 1858 campaign for a seat in the United States Senate, Abraham Lincoln of Illinois delivered his "House Divided" speech, the most important address of his pre-presidential career. Lincoln described his nation as a house divided—half slave and half free—and he warned that a nation constructed in this fashion cannot long last. Below is an excerpt from that speech.

"A house divided against itself cannot stand."

I believe this government cannot endure, permanently half *slave* and half *free.*

I do not expect the Union to be *dissolved*—I do not expect the house to *fall*—but I *do* expect that it will cease to be divided.

It will become *all* one thing, or *all* the other.

Either the *opponents* of slavery, will arrest the further spread of it, and place it where the public mind shall rest in the belief that it is in course of ultimate extinction; or its *advocates* will push it forward, till it shall become alike lawful in *all* the States, *old* as well as *new*—*North* as well as *South.*

Abraham Lincoln, *Selected Speeches and Writings.* New York: Viking Books, 1992.

Document 13: John Brown, "the meteor of war"

In the poem "The Portent," Herman Melville identifies John Brown as "the meteor" of the Civil War. Brown was executed in Virginia in De-

cember 1859 after trying to ignite a slave revolt in Harpers Ferry, Virginia. The poem was included in a collection by Melville titled Battle-Pieces and Aspects of the War, *published in 1866.*

Hanging from the beam,
  Slowly swaying (such the law),
Gaunt the shadow on your green,
  Shenandoah!
The cut is on the crown
(Lo, John Brown),
And the stabs shall heal no more.

Hidden in the cap
  Is the anguish none can draw;
So your future veils its face,
  Shenandoah!
But the streaming beard is shown
(Weird John Brown),
The meteor of the war.

Herman Melville, *Battle-Pieces and Aspects of the War,* 1866; reprint, New York: Thomas Yoseloff, 1963.

Document 14: Abraham Lincoln's Campaign Song

Songwriter Jesse Hutchinson composed a song titled "Lincoln and Liberty" for Abraham Lincoln's 1860 presidential campaign. The song painted Lincoln as an abolitionist, though he claimed that he wanted only to curtail the spread of slavery, not to abolish it in the South where it had long existed. The song helped convince the South that a Lincoln presidency would be a threat to slavery. Indeed, several Southern states voted to secede from the Union after Lincoln's election.

Hurrah for the choice of the nation,
Our chieftain so brave and so true;
We'll go for the great reformation,
For Lincoln and liberty too.

We'll go for the son of Kentucky,
The hero of hoosierdom through,
The pride of the suckers so lucky,
For Lincoln and liberty too.

Then up with the banner so glorious
The star-spangled red, white and blue

We'll fight 'til our banner's victorious
For Lincoln and liberty too.

Come all of you friends of the nation;
Attend to humanity's call;
Come aid in the slaves' liberation,
And roll on the liberty ball.

And roll on the liberty ball,
And roll on the liberty ball;
Come aid in the slaves' liberation,
And roll on the liberty ball.

Songs of the Civil War. Columbia Records, 1991.

Document 15: An Ordinance of Secession

In December 1860, just several weeks after the election of Abraham Lincoln, the South Carolina legislature passed the following ordinance of secession.

TO DISSOLVE THE UNION BETWEEN THE STATE OF SOUTH CAROLINA AND OTHER STATES UNITED WITH HER UNDER THE COMPACT ENTITLED "THE CONSTITUTION OF THE UNITED STATES OF AMERICA,"
We, the People of the State of South Carolina, in Convention assembled, do declare and ordain, and it is hereby declared and ordained,

That the ordinance adopted by us in Convention, on the twenty-third day of May, in the year of our Lord one thousand seven hundred and eighty-eight, whereby the Constitution of the United States of America was ratified, and also, all Acts and parts of the General Assembly of this State, ratifying amendments of the said Constitution, are hereby repealed; and that the union now subsisting between South Carolina and other States, under the name of "The United States of America," is hereby dissolved.

Quoted in Richard B. Harwell, ed., *The Confederate Reader.* New York: David McKay Company, 1957.

Document 16: A Southerner Withdraws from the Union

In January 1861, several weeks before Abraham Lincoln became president, Senator Jefferson Davis of Mississippi wrote to former president Franklin Pierce, whom Davis served as secretary of war, to explain his decision to withdraw from the Union, as the state of Mississippi had already done. Davis would become president of the Confederate States of America.

I have often sadly turned my thoughts to you during the troublous times through which we have been passing and now I come to the hard task of announcing to you that the hour is at hand which closes my connection with the United States, for the independence and Union of which my Father bled and in the service of which I have sought to emulate the example he set for my guidance. Mississippi not as a matter of choice but of necessity has resolved to enter the trial of secession. Those who have driven her to this alternative threaten to deprive her of the right to require that her government shall rest on the consent of the governed, to substitute foreign force for domestic support, to reduce a state to a condition from which the colony rose. . . .

When Lincoln comes in he will have but to continue in the path of his predecessor to inaugurate a civil war and, leave a soi disant democratic administration responsible for the fact.

Quoted in Dunbar Rowland, ed., *Jefferson Davis: Constitutionalist, His Letters, Papers and Speeches.* Jackson: Mississippi Department of Archives and History, 1923.

Document 17: Lincoln's First Inaugural Address: A Plea for Reconciliation

In his First Inaugural Address, delivered on March 4, 1861, President Abraham Lincoln tried to assure the Southern slave states, seven of which had already voted to secede from the Union, that he had no intention of trying to abolish slavery in the states in which it already existed. He concluded his inaugural address with a lyrical plea for reconciliation. The South ignored Lincoln's pleas for reconciliation, and the Civil War began a month later.

Apprehension seems to exist among the people of the Southern States, that by the accession of a Republican Administration, their property, and their peace and personal security, are to be endangered. There has never been any reasonable cause for such apprehension. Indeed, the most ample evidence to the contrary has all the while existed, and been open to their inspection. It is found in nearly all the published speeches of him who now addresses you. I do but quote from one of those speeches when I declare that "I have no purpose, directly or indirectly, to interfere with the institution of slavery in the States where it exists. I believe I have no lawful right to do so, and I have no inclination to do so." Those who nominated and elected me did so with full knowledge that I made this, and many similar declarations, and had never recanted them.

I am loth to close. We are not enemies, but friends. We must not be enemies. Though passion may have strained, it must not break our bonds of affection. The mystic chords of memory, stretching from every battle-field, and patriot grave, to every living heart and hearthstone, all over this broad land, will yet swell the chorus of Union, when again touched, as surely they will be, by the better angels of our nature.

Abraham Lincoln, *Selected Speeches and Writings*. New York: Viking Books, 1992.

Document 18: The War Begins

Throughout the Civil War, Mary Chesnut of South Carolina kept a diary that recorded national and personal events during the conflict. In these two excerpts from her diary, Chesnut records the war's opening salvo—the South Carolina militia's successful attack on Fort Sumter in Charleston Harbor. After a day-long siege, Union major Robert Anderson surrendered the fort.

April 13, 1861

A lull after the storm. Last night we were jubilant. "No one hurt." No battery even injured—& Anderson has two guns spoiled & his fort injured. To day—the enemy's fort has been repeatedly on fire. Still his guns fire regularly. Still vessels are off the bar—& war is at our doors—but 'tho' we hear the firing we feel so differently—because we feel that our merciful God has protected our men—& we pray with faith.

April 15, 1861

Saturday last was a great day. I saw my husband carried by a mob to tell [Confederate] Gen Beauregard the news that Fort Sumter had surrendered—he followed Louis Wigfall to Fort Sumter after a few minutes' interval, then returned with the news of the surrender & carried fire Engines to Fort Sumter. Our men cheered madly when Anderson continued his firing after he was blazing with houses on fire. . . . Mrs. Joe Heyward, Mrs. Preston, Mrs. Wigfall & I drove on the battery in an open carriage. So gay it was—crowded & the tents & cannons.

Quoted in C. Vann Woodward and Elisabeth Muhlenfeld, eds., *The Private Mary Chesnut: The Unpublished Civil War Diaries*. New York: Oxford University Press, 1984.

Document 19: Pressure on Lincoln to Free the Slaves

During the first two years of the Civil War, abolitionists pressured President Abraham Lincoln to free the slaves and to allow African Americans to enlist in the Union army. Before January 1, 1863, Lincoln steadfastly refused to do both, which resulted in criticism from abolitionists like Frederick Douglass. In this excerpt from an 1862 editorial in Douglass' newspaper, Douglass criticizes Lincoln's policy on abolition.

I come now to the policy of President Lincoln in reference to slavery. An administration without a policy is confessedly an administration without brains. . . . I do not undertake to say that the present administration has no policy, but if it has, the people have a right to know what it is, and to approve or disapprove of it as they shall deem it wise or unwise. . . .

Now what has been the tendency of his acts since he became Commander in chief of the army and navy? I do not hesitate to say, that whatever may have been his intentions, the action of President Lincoln has been calculated in a marked and decided way to shield and protect slavery from the very blows which its horrible crimes have loudly and persistently invited. He has scornfully rejected the policy of arming the slaves, a policy naturally suggested and enforced by the nature and necessity of the war. He has steadily refused to proclaim, as he had the constitutional and moral right to proclaim, complete emancipation to all the slaves of rebels who should make their way into the lines of our army. He has repeatedly interfered with and arrested the antislavery policy of some of his most earnest and reliable generals. He has assigned to the most important positions, generals who are notoriously pro-slavery, and hostile to the party and principles which raised him to power.—He has permitted rebels to recapture their runaway slaves in sight of the capital. . . . It is from such action as this, that we must infer the policy of the Administration. To my mind that policy is simply and solely to reconstruct the union on the old and corrupting basis of compromise, by which slavery shall retain all the power that it ever had, with the full assurance of gaining more, according to its future necessities.

Quoted in Richard A. Long, ed., *Black Writers and the American Civil War.* Secaucus, New Jersey: Blue & Grey Press, 1988.

Document 20: The Emancipation Proclamation

On January 1, 1863, President Abraham Lincoln signed the Emancipation Proclamation, which freed the slaves in the rebellious states and invited African Americans to enlist in the Union army. Below is an excerpt from Lincoln's decree.

And by virtue of the power, and for the purpose aforesaid, I do order and declare that all persons held as slaves within said designated States, and parts of States, are, and henceforward shall be free; and that the Executive government of the United States, including the military and naval authorities thereof, will recognize and maintain the freedom of said persons. . . .

And I further declare and make known, that such persons of suitable condition, will be received into the armed service of the United States to garrison forts, positions, stations, and other places, and to man vessels of all sorts in said service.

Abraham Lincoln, *Selected Speeches and Writings.* New York: Viking Books, 1992.

Document 21: A Union Soldier Celebrates Victories at Gettysburg and Vicksburg

Elisha Hunt Rhodes fought in the Second Rhode Island regiment and saw action in twenty major battles, including Bull Run, Antietam, Fredericksburg, Gettysburg, the Wilderness, and Petersburg. After the Union victory at Gettysburg, Rhodes recorded in his diary his feelings of jubilation upon hearing that General Robert E. Lee had retreated into Virginia and that the Union army, on the same day, had achieved victory at Vicksburg, Mississippi. These two victories helped turned the tide of the war in the North's favor.

July 4th 1863

Was ever the Nation's Birthday celebrated in such a way before. The morning the 2nd R.I. was sent out to the front and found that during the night General Lee and his Rebel Army had fallen back. It was impossible to march across the field without stepping upon dead or wounded men, while horses and broken Artillery lay on every side. We advanced to a sunken road (Emmitsburg Road) where we deployed as skirmishers and lay down behind a bank of earth. . . .

July 5th 1863

Glorious news! We have won the victory, thank God, and the Rebel Army is fleeing Virginia. We have news that Vicksburg has fallen. We have thousands of prisoners, and they seem to be stupefied with the news. This morning our Corps (the 6th) started in pursuit of Lee's Army. We have had rain and the roads are bad, so we move slow. Every house we see is a hospital, and the road is covered with the arms and equipments thrown away by the rebels.

Robert Hunt Rhodes, ed., *All for the Union: The Civil War Diary and Letters of Elisha Hunt Rhodes.* New York: Orion Books, 1985.

Document 22: A Southerner Senses Defeat

The writer William Gilmore Simms of South Carolina defended the South's cause in newspaper editorials and other writings. His optimism about the South's cause gave way, late in 1864, to an extreme pessimism as Union general William T. Sherman's army cut a path through Georgia and commenced his famous March to Sea. In this letter to his friend Edward Woodlands, Simms expresses his despair. The war, and the Confederate quest for independence, would end four months later.

I write with painful effort. I have been too much staggered by recent events to command the resources of my mind. I cannot *will* myself to thought. I can only fold hands, & wonder, and perhaps pray. What awaits us in the future, is perhaps foreshown to us by the Past, of trial and loss and suffering. Or it may be that God designs that we should surrender in sacrifice our choicest professions, that we may become worthy of the great boon of future Independence. Yet while I write, and hope, and pray, the day grows more clouded. I trembled & had sore misgivings when [Confederate General] Johnson was removed from the army, & [General] Hood put in his place. I predicted evil then to your father & to others. He concurred with me. And when Hood removed from Sherman's front, I then declared my opinion that if Sherman had the requisite audacity—it did not need Genius,—he would achieve the greatest of his successes, by turning his back on the enemy in his rear, & march boldly forward towards the Atlantic coast. I fear that such is his purpose. If so,—what have we to oppose him? I dare not look upon the prospect before us. It may become necessary for you, for me, & all to prepare as we can, for the overrunning of Carolina! All's very dark.

Louis P. Masur, *"The Real War Will Never Get into the Books": Selections from Writers During the Civil War.* New York: Oxford University Press, 1991.

Document 23: A Song for a War-Weary Nation

During the Civil War, Patrick Sarsfield Gilmore, a band leader who was a member of the Union army, composed the song "When Johnny Comes Marching Home." The song became popular in both the North and the South as the casualties mounted on both sides and the folks at home grew weary of war.

When Johnny comes marching home again,
  Hurrah! Hurrah!
We'll give him a hearty welcome then,
  Hurrah! Hurrah!

The men will cheer, the boys will shout,
The ladies they will all turn out.

Chorus—
And we'll all feel gay,
When Johnny comes marching home.

The old church-bell will peal with joy,
   Hurrah! Hurrah!
To welcome home our darling boy,
   Hurrah! Hurrah!
The village lads and lasses say
With roses they will strew the way.

Lois Hill, ed., *Poems and Songs of the Civil War.* New York: Fairfax Press, 1990.

Document 24: A Hope for Reconciliation

The poet Walt Whitman spent most of the war working as a volunteer nurse in army hospitals in Washington, D.C. After the war, Whitman published Drum-Taps, *a collection of poems based upon the war. The poem "Reconciliation" expresses Whitman's hope that North and South will reconcile their differences and live together as countrymen after the war.*

Word over all, beautiful as the sky,
Beautiful that war and all its deeds of carnage must in time be
   utterly lost,
That the hands of the sisters Death and Night incessantly softly
   wash again, and ever again, this soil'd world;
For my enemy is dead, a man divine as myself is dead,
I look where he lies white-faced and still in the coffin—I draw
   near,
Bend down and touch lightly with my lips the white face in the
   coffin.

Walt Whitman, *Leaves of Grass,* 1892; reprint, New York: Bantam Books, 1983.

Document 25: The Thirteenth Amendment

Early in 1865, Congress approved the Thirteenth Amendment to the Constitution, printed in full below. The amendment then needed approval by three-fourths of the individual state legislatures, a process completed in December 1865. The amendment outlaws slavery in the United States and its territories.

Section 1 Neither slavery nor involuntary servitude, except as a

punishment for crime whereof the party shall have been duly convicted, shall exist within the United States, or any place subject to
their jurisdiction.

Section 2 Congress shall have power to enforce this article by
appropriate legislation.

The Thirteenth Amendment to the United States Constitution, 1865.

Chronology

1619
The first slaves are brought to America on a ship that lands in Jamestown, Virginia. Slavery spreads throughout America.

1776
Thirteen American colonies declare independence from Great Britain. The colonies call themselves "free and independent states."

1788
The U.S. Constitution is ratified. The document prohibits the individual states from passing laws to protect or abet runaway slaves.

1793
Eli Whitney patents the cotton gin. During the next three decades, cotton becomes the South's most important crop.

1820
Congress resolves a crisis between the Northern free states and Southern slave states by passing the Missouri Compromise, which admits Missouri and Maine to the Union and outlaws slavery in U.S. territories north of the 36° 30' latitude mark.

1831
On January 1, William Lloyd Garrison, a Massachusetts abolitionist, begins publication of the *Liberator*, an antislavery newspaper. The newspaper gains a wide audience.

In August, Nat Turner leads an unsuccessful slave rebellion in Southampton, Virginia. Southerners blame Northerners like William Lloyd Garrison for inciting the slaves.

1833
Garrison and his followers establish the American Anti-Slavery Society.

1850
Congress resolves another crisis between the North and South by passing the Compromise of 1850, which admits California into the Union and includes a strict Fugitive Slave Law.

1852
Harriet Beecher Stowe publishes the antislavery novel *Uncle Tom's Cabin.*

1854
Congress passes the Kansas-Nebraska Act, which allows residents of Kansas and Nebraska to decide whether their territories will enter the Union as slave or free states. A civil war between proslavery and antislavery settlers breaks out in Kansas, which becomes known as "bleeding Kansas."

The Republican Party is formed as a result of the passage of the Kansas-Nebraska legislation. The party opposes the spread of slavery to U.S. territories.

1859
John Brown attempts to ignite a slave rebellion at Harpers Ferry, Virginia. Brown is convicted of treason and murder and executed. Southerners accuse the Republican party of supporting Brown's effort.

1860
In November, Republican Abraham Lincoln is elected president. A month later, in reaction to Lincoln's election, the South Carolina legislature votes to secede from the Union.

1861
In January and February, six Southern states follow South Carolina's lead by passing secession ordinances.

On February 8, representatives from the seven Southern states that withdrew from the Union meet in Montgomery, Alabama, and form the Confederate States of America. Jefferson Davis is elected president of the Confederacy.

On March 4, Lincoln is inaugurated as president. In his inaugural address, he urges the South to remain in the Union and pledges not to attempt to abolish slavery.

The Civil War begins on April 12, when South Carolina's militia opens fire on Fort Sumner, a U.S. battery in Charleston harbor. Four more Southern states vote to secede from the Union in the wake of the attack on Fort Sumner.

On July 21, Confederate forces win the first major battle of the Civil War. The Battle of Bull Run, fought in Manassas, Virginia, concludes with Union troops retreating in disarray toward Washington.

1862

In May, Union General George B. McClellan's Peninsula Campaign fails to achieve its goal of capturing Richmond, the Confederate capital. General Robert E. Lee, who thwarted McClellan's advance, is named commander of the Army of Northern Virginia.

At the end of August, the South scores another convincing victory at the Second Battle of Bull Run. The Confederacy hopes for recognition by Great Britain and France.

On September 17, at the Battle of Antietam, fought near Sharpsburg, Maryland, General McClellan stops General Lee's advance into Northern territory in one of the bloodiest engagements of the war.

Five days after the Battle of Antietam, President Lincoln issues the Preliminary Emancipation Proclamation, notifying the South that slaves will be freed in the rebellious states on January 1, 1863.

On December 13, Union forces are convincingly defeated at the Battle of Fredericksburg.

1863

On January 1, President Lincoln issues the Emancipation Proclamation, freeing slaves in the rebellious states not in Union control.

In early July, the South suffers crippling battlefield setbacks at Gettysburg, Pennsylvania, and Vicksburg, Mississippi. At the Battle of Gettysburg, Union forces halt Lee's second advance into Northern territory. Union General Ulysses S. Grant's capture of Vicksburg puts the Mississippi River in Union control and cuts the Confederacy in two.

1864

In September, Union General William T. Sherman commences his March to the Sea by capturing Atlanta, Georgia. In November, he captures Savannah.

In November, President Lincoln is reelected, dashing the South's hope that Lincoln's defeat might prompt a peace treaty and recognition of the Confederacy.

1865

On January 31, Congress votes to approve the Thirteenth Amendment to the U.S. Constitution, which prohibits slavery throughout the United States and its territories. The amendment becomes part of the Constitution in December after approval by the requisite three-fourth of the states.

On April 2, Richmond, Virginia, falls to Union forces. President Lincoln visits the former Confederate capital.

On April 9, General Lee surrenders to General Grant at Appomattox Courthouse, Virginia. Within six weeks, all remaining Confederate forces will surrender, ending the Civil War.

On April 14, President Lincoln is shot at Ford's Theatre in Washington. He dies the next morning.

For Further Research

Biographies of Prominent Civil War–Era Individuals

Eaton Clement, *Jefferson Davis*. New York: Free Press, 1977.

William J. Cooper, *Jefferson Davis: American*. New York: Alfred A. Knopf, 2000.

Richard N. Current, *The Lincoln Nobody Knows*. New York: McGraw Hill, 1958.

Don E. Fehrenbacher, *Prelude to Greatness: Lincoln in the 1850s*. Stanford, CA: Stanford University Press, 1962.

Douglas Southall Freeman, *R.E. Lee: A Biography*. 4 vols. New York: Charles Scribner's Sons, 1935.

Alan T. Nolan, *Lee Considered: General Robert E. Lee and Civil War History*. Chapel Hill: University of North Carolina Press, 1991.

Stephen B. Oates, *Abraham Lincoln: The Man Behind the Myths*. New York: Harper & Row, 1984.

Irving Werstein, *Abraham Lincoln Versus Jefferson Davis*. New York: Crowell, 1959.

Douglas L. Wilson, *Honor's Voice: The transformation of Abraham Lincoln*. New York: Alfred A. Knopf, 1998.

Histories of the Civil War Era

James L. Abrahamson, *The Men of Secession and Civil War, 1859–1861*. Wilmington, DE: Scholarly Resources, 2000.

William L. Barney, *Battleground for the Union: The Era of the Civil War and Reconstruction, 1848–1877*. Englewood Cliffs, NJ: Prentice-Hall, 1990.

———, *Flawed Victory: A New Perspective on the Civil War*. New York: Praeger, 1975.

Richard E. Beringer, et al, *Why the South Lost the Civil War*. Athens: University of Georgia Press, 1986.

Bruce Catton, *The Centennial History of the Civil War*. 3 vols. Garden City, NY: Doubleday, 1965.

———, *Reflections on the Civil War*. Garden City, NY: Doubleday, 1981.

William C. Davis, *An Honorable Defeat: The Last Days of the Confederate Government.* New York: Harcourt, 2001.

——, *The Lost Cause: Myths and Realities of the Confederacy.* Lawrence: University Press of Kansas, 1996.

Shelby Foote, *The Civil War: A Narrative.* 3 vols. New York: Random House, 1974.

Joseph L. Harsh, *Confederate Tide Rising: Robert E. Lee and the Making of Southern Strategy, 1861–1862.* Kent, OH: Kent State University Press, 1998.

John Macdonald, *Great Battles of the Civil War.* New York: Macmillan, 1988.

James M. McPherson, *Crossroads of Freedom: Antietam.* New York: Oxford University Press, 2002.

——, *Battle Cry of Freedom: The Civil War Era.* New York: Oxford University Press, 1988.

——, *Drawn with the Sword: Reflections on the American Civil War.* New York: Oxford University Press, 1996.

Phillip Shaw Paludan, *"A People's Contest": The Union and the Civil War, 1861–1865.* New York: Harper & Row, 1988.

Peter J. Parish, *The American Civil War.* New York: Holmes & Meier, 1975.

J.G. Randall and David Donald, *The Civil War and Reconstruction.* Boston: D.C. Heath, 1961.

James A. Rawley, *Turning Points of the Civil War.* Lincoln: University of Nebraska Press, 1966.

Geoffrey C. Ward, Ric Burns, and Ken Burns, *The Civil War: An Illustrated History.* New York: Alfred A. Knopf, 1990.

Robert Penn Warren, *The Legacy of the Civil War: Meditations on the Centennial.* New York: Random House, 1961.

Bell Irvin Wiley, *The Road to Appomattox.* New York: Atheneum, 1975.

Jay Winik, *April 1865: The Month That Saved America.* New York: HarperCollins, 2001.

Texts Containing Primary-Source Documents

Louisa May Alcott, *Hospital Sketches.* Chester, CT: Applewood, 1990.

Henry Steele Commager, ed., *The Blue and the Gray: The Story of the Civil War as Told by Participants*. New York: Bobbs-Merrill, 1950.

William C. Davis, ed., *Diary of a Confederate Soldier: John S. Jackman of the Orphan Brigade*. Columbia: University of South Carolina Press, 1990.

William Dudley, ed., *The Civil War: Opposing Viewpoints*. San Diego: Greenhaven Press, 1995.

———, *Slavery: Opposing Viewpoints*. San Diego: Greenhaven Press, 1992.

Lois Hill, *Poems and Songs of the Civil War*. New York: Fairfax Press, 1990.

Abraham Lincoln, *Selected Speeches and Writings*. New York: Vintage Books, 1992.

Richard A. Long, ed., *Black Writers and the American Civil War*. Secaucus, NJ: The Blue & Gray Press, 1988.

Mason Lowance, ed., *Against Slavery: An Abolitionist Reader*. New York: Penguin Books, 2000.

Louis P. Masur, ed., *The Real War Will Never Get in the Books: Selections from Writers During the Civil War*. New York: Oxford University Press, 1993.

Robert Hunt Rhodes, ed., *All for the Union: The Civil War Diary and Letters of Elisha Hunt Rhodes*. New York: Orion Books, 1985.

Thomas Streissguth, ed., *The Civil War: The South*. San Diego: Greenhaven Press, 2001.

C. Vann Woodward and Elisabeth Muhlenfeld, eds., *The Private Mary Chesnut: The Unpublished Civil War Diaries*. New York: Oxford University Press, 1984.

Index